MW01178621

Being One
with the Lord
in His Move
for the
Universal
Spreading of
the Church
as the
Testimony
of Jesus

Witness Lee

The Holy Word for Morning Revival

Living Stream Ministry
Anaheim, CA • www.lsm.org

First Edition, June 2009.

ISBN 978-0-7363-4068-7

Published by

Living Stream Ministry
2431 W. La Palma Ave., Anaheim, CA 92801 U.S.A.
P. O. Box 2121, Anaheim, CA 92814 U.S.A.

Printed in the United States of America

09 10 11 12 13 / 7 6 5 4 3 2 1

Contents

2009 Memorial Day Weekend Conference

BEING ONE WITH THE LORD IN HIS MOVE FOR THE UNIVERSAL SPREADING OF THE CHURCH AS THE TESTIMONY OF JESUS

Preface

1. This book is intended as an aid to believers in developing a daily time of morning revival with the Lord in His word. At the same time, it provides a limited review of the Memorial Day weekend conference held in Philadelphia, Pennsylvania, May 22-25, 2009. Through intimate contact with the Lord in His word, the believers can be constituted with life and truth and thereby equipped to prophesy in the meetings of the church unto the building up of the Body of Christ.

2. The entire content of this book is taken primarily from the published conference outlines, the text and footnotes of the Recovery Version of the Bible, selections from the writings of Witness Lee and Watchman Nee, and *Hymns,* all of which are published by Living Stream Ministry.

3. The book is divided into weeks. One conference message is covered per week. Each week presents first the message outline, followed by six daily portions, a hymn, and then some space for writing. The message outline has been divided into days, corresponding to the six daily portions. Each daily portion covers certain points and begins with a section entitled "Morning Nourishment." This section contains selected verses and a short reading that can provide rich spiritual nourishment through intimate fellowship with the Lord. The "Morning Nourishment" is followed by a section entitled "Today's Reading," a longer portion of ministry related to the day's main points. Each day's portion concludes with a short list of references for further reading and some space for the saints to make notes concerning their spiritual inspiration, enlightenment, and enjoyment to serve as a reminder of what they have received of the Lord that day.

4. The space provided at the end of each week is for composing a short prophecy. This prophecy can be composed by considering all of our daily notes, the "harvest" of our inspirations during the week, and preparing a main point

with some sub-points to be spoken in the church meetings for the organic building up of the Body of Christ.

5. Following the last week in this volume, we have provided reading schedules for both the Old and New Testaments in the Recovery Version with footnotes. These schedules are arranged so that one can read through both the Old and New Testaments of the Recovery Version with footnotes in two years.

6. As a practical aid to the saints' feeding on the Word throughout the day, we have provided verse cards at the end of the volume, which correspond to each day's scripture reading. These may be removed and carried along as a source of spiritual enlightenment and nourishment in the saints' daily lives.

7. The conference message outlines were compiled by Living Stream Ministry from the writings of Witness Lee and Watchman Nee. The outlines, footnotes, and references in the Recovery Version of the Bible are by Witness Lee. All of the other references cited in this publication are from the published ministry of Witness Lee and Watchman Nee.

Memorial Day Weekend Conference

(May 22-25, 2009)

General Subject:

Being One with the Lord in His Move for the Universal Spreading of the Church as the Testimony of Jesus

Banners:

The coordination of the believers as members
of the Body of Christ results in the corporate
expression of Christ, the move of God on earth,
the administration of God on the throne, and
the fulfillment of God's eternal purpose.

For the universal spreading of the church
as the testimony of Jesus, we need to experience,
enjoy, and grow Christ as the tree of life and
plant "church trees" for the corporate
expression of the Triune God as life.

We need to live the life of the altar and the tent,
offering all that we are and have to God
for His purpose and migrating to spread the church life
from city to city, from country to country, and
from continent to continent until there are
local churches all over the earth.

We need to have fellowship unto the furtherance
of the gospel until the Lord comes back and
spread the truths of the gospel of God's eternal economy
throughout the whole inhabited earth
for a testimony to all the nations
before the end of this age.

**The Wind, the Cloud, the Fire, and the Electrum
and the Coordination of the Four Living Creatures
for God's Expression, Move, and Administration**

Scripture Reading: Ezek. 1:4-16, 26

Day 1   **I. The spiritual history of every normal Christian
should be a continual cycle involving the experience of God as the wind, the cloud, the fire,
and the electrum (Ezek. 1:4):**

A. Whenever God visits us and revives us, His Spirit
blows on us like a mighty wind to bring a spiritual
storm into our life, into our work, and into our
church, causing us to be dissatisfied and concerned
about our spiritual condition and to have a turn in
our spiritual life (v. 4).

B. The cloud is a figure of God as the Spirit abiding
with His people and covering them in order to care
for them and show favor to them (v. 4; Exo. 13:21;
40:34-35).

Day 2   C. The fire signifies God's burning and sanctifying
power; the more the fire of the Holy Spirit burns
in us, the more we are purified and enlightened
(Ezek. 1:4; Deut. 4:24; Heb. 12:29).

D. The electrum, composed of the elements of gold
and silver, signifies the Lamb-God, the redeeming
God (Ezek. 1:4; Rev. 22:1):

1. The more we experience the wind, the cloud,
and the fire, the more the electrum is constituted into our being, making us a people who
are filled with the Triune God and who manifest His glory (Eph. 3:16-17, 21).

2. The issue of the spiritual transactions involving the blowing wind, the covering cloud, and
the purifying fire is the glowing electrum—
the radiant expression of the redeeming God.

Day 3   **II. The more we experience God as the blowing
wind, the overshadowing cloud, the burning
fire, and the glowing electrum, the more we**

are enlivened with the divine life to become
the four living creatures (Ezek. 1:5a):

A. The four living creatures are reckoned not as individuals but as a group, one entity.

B. That the four living creatures bear the likeness of
   a man and that God on the throne also bears the
   appearance of a man indicates that God's central
   thought and His arrangement are related to man
   (vv. 5b, 26; Gen. 1:26; Psa. 8:4-8):
   1. According to the vision unveiled in Ezekiel 1,
      man is the means for God to manifest His
      glory, for God to move on the earth, and for
      God to administrate on the throne.
   2. God uses the wind, the cloud, the fire, and the
      electrum to enliven us in order to gain man
      as the means for His manifestation, move,
      and administration.

Day 4 III. **Ezekiel 1:11b-14 conveys a clear picture of the
       coordination of the living creatures—a por-
       trait of the proper church life with the coordi-
       nation of the members of the Body of Christ:**

A. The joining of the two wings (eagle's wings) of the
   living creatures is for their corporate moving in
   coordination (v. 11b):
   1. The wings of an eagle signify the grace, strength,
      and power of God applied to us (Exo. 19:4; Isa.
      40:31; 2 Cor. 1:12; 4:7; 12:9).
   2. The eagle's wings are the means by which the
      living creatures are coordinated and move as
      one; their coordination is not in themselves
      but in God and by the divine grace, strength,
      and power (cf. Exo. 26:26-29).

B. The move of the living creatures is not individual but corporate, the move of one entity in coordination; this is a beautiful picture of the coordination in the church as the Body of Christ, in which
   each member has his particular position and function, or ministry (Ezek. 1:12; Rom. 12:4-8; 1 Cor.
   12:14-30; Eph. 4:7-16).

Day 5　　C. The issue of the coordination of the living creatures is that they become burning coals, with the holy God as a consuming fire burning among them and within them; that both the Lord on the throne and the living creatures have the appearance of fire indicates that the living creatures are the expression of the Lord (Ezek. 1:13, 26; Heb. 12:29).

D. The living creatures, having a proper coordination, will not walk but run, because they have the power and the impact (Ezek. 1:14).

E. The coordination of the believers as members of the Body of Christ results in the corporate expression of Christ, in the move of God on the earth, and in the administration of God on the throne, thus affording God a way to manifest His glory and accomplish His eternal purpose and plan (vv. 4-12, 26).

Day 6　　**IV. In the book of Ezekiel God's economy and God's move in His economy are signified by a great wheel (v. 15; Eph. 1:10; 3:9; 1 Tim. 1:4):**

A. The hub of this great wheel signifies Christ as the center of God's economy; the rim signifies Christ's counterpart, the church, which consummates in the New Jerusalem; and the spokes of the wheel spreading from the hub to the rim signify the many believers as the members of Christ (Col. 1:15-18; Eph. 5:30).

B. The appearing of the wheels on the earth beside the living creatures indicates that God's move on earth follows the coordination of the four living creatures (Ezek. 1:15).

C. The wheels being for the four faces of the living creatures indicates that if we would have the Lord's move, we must first live out the Lord, expressing Him (v. 15; Phil. 1:20-21a).

D. All four wheels have the same appearance; this indicates that the move of the Lord has the same appearance in every church (1 Cor. 4:17; 7:17; 11:16).

E. A wheel within a wheel indicates that in the move of the living creatures there is the move of the Lord; the inner wheel, the Lord as the hub, is the source of the power for the moving of the outer wheel, the church as the rim (Ezek. 1:16).

Morning Nourishment

Ezek. And I looked, and there came a storm wind from the
1:4　north, a great cloud and a fire flashing incessantly;
and there was a brightness around it, and from the
midst of it there was *something* like the sight of
electrum, from the midst of the fire.

Exo. Then the cloud covered the Tent of Meeting, and
40:34　the glory of Jehovah filled the tabernacle.

My burden is to point out that the wind, the cloud, the fire, and
the electrum [in Ezekiel 1] should be a Christian's spiritual life
story. Throughout our whole Christian life, our spiritual experiences should be a continual cycle involving these four matters.

[This] is absolutely not a theory but something of spiritual experience. If a person has never experienced the wind, the cloud, the
fire, and the electrum, that person surely is not a normal Christian.
A...person may have a little doctrinal knowledge of the truth concerning salvation and then be baptized in a formal way without
having any experience of the wind, the cloud, the fire, and the
electrum. A genuinely saved person is one who has had spiritual
transactions with God, one who has experienced the blowing of
the wind and the covering of the cloud. (*Life-study of Ezekiel*, p. 37)

Today's Reading

Our spiritual experiences always begin with a spiritual storm.
According to church history, throughout all the generations the
Spirit of God has blown like a mighty wind to move people to
repent of their sins, to believe in the Lord Jesus for their regenera-
tion, to give up the world in order to follow the Lord, and to be des-
perate in heart and burning in spirit to serve the Lord....Have you
not sensed the wind of God blowing upon you? Have you not been
touched by the Spirit of God? Have you not sensed, at least once in
your life, that a certain power—the stormy wind from God—was
moving upon you, causing you to hate sin, to have a different atti-
tude toward the world, or to change your view concerning your
life? If you have never had such experiences, you need to look to
the Lord and pray for His wind from the north to blow upon you.

Actually, a stormy wind blows upon us at every turn in our spiritual life. This stormy wind is God Himself blowing upon us to bring a storm into our life, into our work, and into our church. It is truly a grace to have storms coming to us from God. As we are following the Lord, we will experience storm after storm....I can testify that every storm is worth recalling. Every storm has become a pleasant remembrance. I believe that when we are in eternity, we will recall the storms that we experienced.

Whenever God visits us and revives us, His Spirit blows upon us like a mighty wind. We need to experience the Spirit in this way—the more, the better and the stronger, the better. I have the deep longing that in these days the Spirit of God would blow strongly upon us like a mighty wind.

The cloud always follows the stormy wind. If we have the wind, we will surely have the cloud, for the cloud is the issue of the blowing of the wind. Like the stormy wind, the cloud signifies the Holy Spirit. When the Holy Spirit touches us, He is like the wind. When the Holy Spirit visits us and overshadows us, He is like the cloud. First, the Holy Spirit blows upon us like the wind to move us, and then He abides with us like a cloud to cover us.

The cloud in Ezekiel 1:4 is a figure of God covering His people. We may use the word *brooding* and say that the cloud was God brooding over His people. The cloud, therefore, was nothing other than the brooding God. God comes as the wind, but He stays as the cloud. By staying as the cloud, He covers us, overshadows us, and broods over us to give us the enjoyment of His presence, thereby producing something of Himself in our daily life. How wonderful! This is the covering God typified by the covering cloud.

Whenever we experience God as the blowing wind, we also have the sense that, after He blows upon us, He remains with us, overshadowing and covering us and brooding over us. This is God as the gracious cloud. (*Life-study of Ezekiel,* pp. 27-30)

Further Reading: Life-study of Ezekiel, msg. 3; *Rising Up to Preach the Gospel,* ch. 3

Enlightenment and inspiration: _____

_____

_____

_____

Morning Nourishment

Deut. For Jehovah your God is a consuming fire, a jealous
4:24 God.

Eph. That Christ may make His home in your hearts
3:17 through faith...

21 To Him be the glory in the church and in Christ Jesus
unto all the generations forever and ever. Amen.

Ezekiel saw that the cloud which overshadowed him was covered with fire flashing continually. This also is a matter which
corresponds to our spiritual experience. When the stormy wind
comes from the Lord and the overshadowing presence of the Lord
remains, we have the sense that something within us is shining,
searching, and burning....Under the shining and searching of the
Lord's presence, we are exposed, and we condemn ourselves and
confess our shortcomings. Then the searching fire will burn away
the negative things within us. (*Life-study of Ezekiel,* p. 32)

Today's Reading

The fire seen by Ezekiel signifies God's burning and sanctifying
power. Everything that does not match God's holy nature and disposition must be burned away. Only what matches His holiness
can pass through His holy fire. This can be confirmed by our spiritual experience. The Holy Spirit comes to convict people regarding
sin, righteousness, and judgment (John 16:8). Whenever the Holy
Spirit touches us and causes us to confess our sins and pray, we
will sense the need to be sanctified and to have all the corruption
purged out of our being. We will realize that anything that does
not match the holiness of God must be burned away. If someone
claims to have been visited by God but has no feeling concerning
his sins and unholiness, that person has not truly been touched
by the Spirit of God. When God visits a person, His holy fire will
come to consume the negative things in him. This burning fire
also causes us to be enlightened. The more the fire of the Holy
Spirit burns in us, the more we will be purified and enlightened.

God comes to us as the blowing wind and stays with us as
the covering cloud. Under His covering we are exposed by His

shining. As we are under His shining, we should confess our need for His burning and then pray for Him to burn away our self, our old nature, our disposition, our worldliness, and our attitudes, goals, aims, motives, and intentions.

God's intention is not simply to burn us and turn us into ashes. God is a good God with a good purpose....[God's] purpose in blowing upon us as the wind, in covering us as the cloud, and in consuming us as the fire...is that out of the fire appears the glowing electrum. The burning of the divine fire is for the manifestation of the electrum.

Electrum is not merely gold nor merely silver but gold mixed with silver....Our God is not merely the divine Being signified by the gold; He is also the redeeming God, signified by the silver. No longer is He just gold—He is electrum, gold mingled with silver.

When we experience the blowing wind, we enjoy the covering cloud, and then we pass through the burning, consuming fire. The result is the glowing electrum, something shining, lovely, precious, and pleasant. As the electrum, the Lord Jesus is the One who has redeemed us and who is everything to us. He is our God, our Lamb, our Redeemer, our jasper, and our sardius. If we consider our spiritual experience, we will realize that the One who dwells within us today is the Lamb-God, the One signified by the electrum.

His wind, His cloud, and His burning fire have made it possible for us to have Him, the redeeming God, within us as the glowing electrum. Now we have Him as the treasure in the earthen vessel (2 Cor. 4:7), and we have thereby become a people of honor and glory. We need to consider how precious and honorable is the Christ who is within us. As the electrum within us, He is the treasure of incomparable worth. This treasure is the issue of the wind, the cloud, and the fire. The more we pass through the wind, the cloud, and the fire, the more the electrum is constituted into our being, making us a people who are filled with the Triune God and who manifest His glory. (*Life-study of Ezekiel,* pp. 32-35)

Further Reading: Life-study of Ezekiel, msg. 4; *Rising Up to Preach the Gospel,* ch. 4

Enlightenment and inspiration: _____
_____
_____
_____

Morning Nourishment

Ezek. And from the midst of it *there came* the likeness of
1:5 four living creatures. And this was their appearance: They had the likeness of a man.
Psa. What is mortal man, that You remember him, and
8:4-5 the son of man, that You visit him? You have made
Him a little lower than angels and have crowned
Him with glory and honor.

We need to pay attention to the first word in Ezekiel 1:5, *and*.
Not only does electrum come out of the fire; something else also
comes out. The wind brings in the cloud; the cloud enfolds the fire;
and the fire produces the electrum plus something else—the four
living creatures. When we experience God as the blowing wind,
the overshadowing cloud, the burning fire, and the electrum, we
become the four living creatures. We were dead, but by experiencing God in this way we become…living.…The more we have the
cycle of the wind, cloud, fire, and electrum, the more living we
become. Every time we are blown upon by God and overshadowed
and consumed and burned by Him, we are enlivened. As a result
we become lively and vibrant. (*Life-study of Ezekiel,* pp. 43-44)

Today's Reading

Daily we need to experience the wind, the cloud, the fire, and
the electrum. Every time we meet the Lord as the wind, the cloud,
the fire, and the electrum, our inner being will be made alive.

The number four symbolizes that we are the people redeemed
from many tribes, tongues, peoples, and nations. In the eyes of
God we are the four living creatures.

The four living creatures are reckoned not as individuals but
as a group. All of them are counted as one entity. Later on we will
see that these living creatures are the corporate expression of the
man on the throne. As such an expression, they express this man
not only in one direction but in the four directions of east, north,
south, and west. This indicates that as the four living creatures
we are not only the unique expression of Christ but also that we
are the complete expression of Christ. We express Christ in every

direction, toward every side. We are the four living creatures expressing Christ in an adequate and complete way.

The main point of Ezekiel 1:5 is that the four living creatures bear the appearance of a man. Verse 26 says that "upon the likeness of the throne was One in appearance like a man, above it." *Man* is a great word in the Bible. God's intention is with man, God's thought is focused on man, and God's heart is set upon man. God's desire is to gain man. The fact that four living creatures bear the appearance of a man and that God on the throne also bears the appearance of a man indicates that God's central thought and His arrangement are related to man.

The vision in Ezekiel 1 reveals three crucial matters concerning the four living creatures' bearing the appearance of a man. First, God's glory is manifested upon them. The manifestation of God's glory depends upon their having the appearance of a man. Where they are, there God's glory is. God's glory is not separate from them, and apart from them God's glory cannot be manifested. Second, these living creatures are the means of God's move. God's move depends on them. When they move, God will move, for His move is with them. Third, the four living creatures...are the means of God's administration. Ezekiel 1 reveals that God is sitting on the throne. God's throne dominates everything on earth and everything recorded in this book. This throne, therefore, is the center of God's administration. However, the center of God's administration depends on the four living creatures having the appearance of a man. Because of this, there is the administration of God's throne....[Thus], we...see that man is the means of God's manifestation,...God's move, and...God's administration. In God's eyes and in God's hands, man has such an important position.

We all need to realize that God's desire is to gain man. God uses the wind, the cloud, the fire, and the electrum to enliven us in order to gain man as the means of His manifestation, move, and administration. (*Life-study of Ezekiel,* pp. 46-47, 50)

Further Reading: Life-study of Ezekiel, msgs. 5-6

Enlightenment and inspiration: _____

_____

_____

_____

Morning Nourishment

Ezek. ...And their wings were spread out upward; two *wings*
1:11-12 of each were joined one to another, and two covered
their bodies. And each went straight forward; wherever the Spirit was to go, they went; they did not turn
as they went.
1 Cor. To a different one faith in the same Spirit, and to an-
12:9 other gifts of healing in the one Spirit.

Ezekiel 1:11b-14 reveals a very clear picture of coordination.
No other verses in the Bible present the matter of coordination in
such a definite and practical way....[Let us now] consider the
coordination of the four living creatures described in this portion
of Ezekiel 1.

[In verse 11] we see that two of their wings are for moving, and
this moving is in coordination. By two of their wings they are
joined to one another, and in this way they are coordinated. As we
have seen, the living creatures use the other two wings to cover
themselves. (*Life-study of Ezekiel*, p. 67)

Today's Reading

In the Old Testament the eagle's wings signify the divine power,
the divine strength, and the divine supply. This indicates that the
coordination of the living creatures is not in themselves. In themselves they do not have the ability to be coordinated. Their coordination is in the divine power, in the divine strength, and in the
divine supply because the eagle's wings are the means for them to
be coordinated with one another. Thus, their coordination does not
depend on themselves; it does not depend on what they are or on
what they can do. Their coordination depends on the eagle's wings.
The eagle's wings are the means by which they are coordinated
and move as one. God Himself is the power and strength, and it is
by this divine power and strength that they are coordinated.

In themselves the living creatures are separate and are individuals, but with the eagle's wings they are coordinated as one
body. This indicates that the coordination among us Christians
is not something of ourselves....Whatever we are in ourselves,

whatever we have in ourselves, and whatever we do in ourselves result not in coordination but in division and separation. However, we have the eagle's wings, and with the eagle's wings we can be one, and we can be coordinated.

It is important for us to realize why we need to be coordinated. We must be coordinated as living creatures in order that Christ may be expressed and manifested. Also, the coordination of the living creatures is for the Lord's move. The Lord moves in the center of the coordination of the living creatures. Furthermore, coordination is the divine administration, the divine government. The throne upon which the Lord is, the throne which is for God's administration, is in the center of this coordination. Thus, the coordination of the living creatures is for the Lord's expression and manifestation, for the Lord's move, and for the divine government.

Now we need to see how the four living creatures are coordinated. Each of the living creatures faces one direction, respectively facing north, south, east, and west. As they face these four directions, two of their wings spread out and touch the adjacent creatures' wings, forming a square. Each of the living creatures uses two of his wings to join with other living creatures.

[In Ezekiel 1:12] we see that every one of the living creatures goes straight forward. They do not turn, but some return, that is, move backward. For instance, while one of the living creatures is moving toward the north, the living creature facing the south must return, moving backward. Thus, one goes straight forward while the opposite creature moves backward. At the same time, the other two living creatures must move sideways. One moves sideways to the left, and the other moves sideways to the right. No matter in which direction the living creatures are moving, there is no need for any one of them to turn. One simply goes straight forward; one returns, moving backward; and the other sides move sideways. This is a beautiful picture of the coordination that we need in the church life. (*Life-study of Ezekiel,* pp. 67-69)

Further Reading: Life-study of Ezekiel, msg. 7; *The Spirit,* ch. 3

Enlightenment and inspiration: _____

_____
_____
_____

Morning Nourishment

Ezek. **As for the likeness of the living creatures, their appear-**
1:13-14 **ance was like burning coals of fire, like the appearance**
of torches; the fire went to and fro among the living
creatures, and the fire was bright; and out of the fire
went forth lightning. And the living creatures ran to
and fro like the appearance of a lightning bolt.

The move of the living creatures [in Ezekiel 1] is not individual but corporate. They move as one entity in coordination. Each of the living creatures faces one direction. As they face these four directions, two of their wings spread out and touch the adjacent creatures' wings, forming a square. When the living creatures move, they do not need to turn; one moves straight forward while the opposite creature moves backward and the other two move sideways (v. 9). This is a beautiful picture of the coordination in the church as the Body of Christ, in which each member has his particular position and function, or ministry (Rom. 12:4-8; 1 Cor. 12:14-30; Eph. 4:7-16). When one member functions, he moves "straight forward" to fulfill his function, and the other members accommodate him by moving in the same direction, some moving "backward" and others moving "sideways." (Ezek. 1:12, footnote 1)

Today's Reading

According to the vision of the four living creatures, the coordination of the believers as members of the Body of Christ results in the corporate expression of God in Christ, in the move of God on the earth, and in the administration of God on the throne, thus affording God a way to manifest His glory and accomplish His eternal purpose and plan. In order to participate in such a coordination, we need to have the spiritual experiences and the practical living symbolized by the details in Ezekiel 1:4-12. (Ezek. 1:12, footnote 1)

The living creatures' following the Spirit indicates that in order to have the genuine coordination, we need to deny ourselves and walk by the Spirit (Gal. 5:16, 25) and according to the spirit (Rom. 8:4). (footnote 2)

The issue of the coordination of the living creatures is that they become burning coals, with the holy God as a consuming fire burning among them and within them (Heb. 12:29; cf. Exo. 3:2 and footnote 2). Furthermore, they become burning torches for shining and enlightening (cf. Rev. 4:5b). The burning of the coals and the enlightening of the torches signify that the sanctifying fire becomes the sanctifying light. That both the Lord on the throne (Ezek. 1:26) and the living creatures have the appearance of fire indicates that the living creatures are the expression of the Lord. (Ezek. 1:13, footnote 1)

The running of the living creatures like lightning indicates that the living creatures, having a proper coordination, being the burning coals and the burning torches, and having the divine fire going to and fro among them, will not walk but run. They run because they have the power and the impact. (Ezek. 1:14, footnote 1)

It is crucial for us to realize that Ezekiel 1 shows us the desire of God's heart and unveils to us the purpose that God wants to accomplish....[This chapter] speaks of God's desire to be expressed in His Son. The four faces of the living creatures signify the complete and adequate expression of Christ. Furthermore, the four living creatures with their four faces signify a coordinated, corporate entity, the corporate Christ (1 Cor. 12:12). This corporate Christ is the corporate expression of God among human beings.

The four living creatures exist for at least three reasons. First, these living creatures are for God's expression....Second, the living creatures are for God's move....Third, the living creatures are for God's administration. Over their heads was the likeness of an expanse, or a firmament (Ezek. 1:22), and "above the expanse that was over their heads was the likeness of a throne" (v. 26). The throne is for God's ruling, God's administration. When God has His expression, move, and administration, He can manifest Himself in His glory and complete His eternal purpose and plan. (*Life-study of Ezekiel,* pp. 79-80)

Further Reading: Life-study of Ezekiel, msg. 8; *New Testament Service,* ch. 3

Enlightenment and inspiration: _____

_____
_____
_____

Morning Nourishment

Ezek.   And as I watched the living creatures, I saw a wheel
1:15-16   upon the earth beside the living creatures, for *each
of their four faces. The appearance of the wheels
and their workmanship were like the sight of beryl.
And the four of them had one likeness; that is, their
appearance and their workmanship were as it were
a wheel within a wheel.

The entire Bible from Genesis to Revelation presents a full
picture of the economy of God (Eph. 1:10; 3:9; 1 Tim. 1:4) and of
God's move on earth to carry out His economy. In the book of
Ezekiel God's economy and God's move in His economy are signified by a wheel. The hub of this great wheel signifies Christ as the
center of God's economy, and the rim signifies Christ's counterpart, the church, which consummates in the New Jerusalem. The
spokes of the wheel spreading from the hub to the rim signify the
many believers as the members of Christ.

The appearing of the wheels on the earth beside the living
creatures indicates that God's move on earth follows the coordination of the four living creatures. The move by a wheel implies
an extraordinary move with a purpose. Furthermore, it implies
that this move is not by our own strength. (Ezek. 1:15, footnote 1)

The wheels being for the four faces of the living creatures indicates that if we would have the Lord's move, we must first live out
the Lord, expressing Him. (footnote 2)

Today's Reading

Ezekiel 1:16b says, "The four of them had one likeness." Here
we are told that all four wheels have the same appearance, the
same likeness. This indicates that the move of the Lord has
the same likeness and appearance in every church. All the moves
bear the same appearance of the Lord. Therefore, the likeness of
all the wheels is the same.

If the church in one locality has a likeness, an appearance,
which is different from the likeness of the church in another locality, something is wrong. The saints in a particular church may

think that they need to build up their own local distinction, that they need to build up something typically and uniquely local. This is contrary to Ezekiel 1, where we are told that all four wheels bear the same likeness.

We should not think that the wheel moving in the United States should bear one appearance and that the wheel moving in other countries should bear a different appearance. In every place and in every country the wheel must bear the same appearance. This does not mean that all the churches should follow one partic-ular church. Rather, all the local churches should be mutual fol-lowers of one another (1 Thes. 2:14).

It is very significant that the wheels look like a wheel within a wheel [Ezek. 1:16c]. When we speak of a wheel, we say that the cir-cumference is the rim, that the center is the hub, and that in be-tween are the spokes. Thus, we have the three main parts of a wheel: the rim, the hub, and the spokes. But in Ezekiel 1 there is no hub, and there are no spokes. Instead, there is a wheel within a wheel.

We may apply this matter of a wheel within a wheel to the church life. If the church is proper and is moving, then within the church's moving there will be the move of the Lord. This means that in our move there is the Lord's move. While we are moving, the Lord is moving in our moving.

The inner wheel is the source of power for the moving. This means that the inner wheel is the "motor" which causes the wheel to move. If our move is genuine, it must be that within our move is the move of the Lord.

The big wheel turns because the little wheel is being turned. In the church life, the Lord Jesus is the hub—the wheel within the wheel—and we are the rim. If the churches do not move with the Lord, they have no way to go on because there is no wheel within the wheel. But when the churches move with the Lord Jesus, He becomes the wheel within the wheel. Nothing can frustrate or stop this kind of move. (*Life-study of Ezekiel,* pp. 95-96, 98-99)

Further Reading: Life-study of Ezekiel, msgs. 9, 12

Enlightenment and inspiration: _____

_____

_____

_____

Hymns, #1200

1   There's a stormy wind a-blowing from the north;
      Let it blow! Let it blow!
    God as our exp'rience will the wind bring forth;
      Let it blow! Let it blow!

> Let it blow! the rushing mighty wind;
>   Let it blow us into life!
> Let it blow! the gracious wind of God;
>   Let it blow us into Christ!

2   There's a hov'ring cloud a-following the wind,
      Covering us! Covering us!
    And the presence of the Lord the cloud does bring,
      Covering us! Covering us!

> Covering us, God's overshadowing cloud—
>   God has come to stay with us.
> Covering us, the gracious cloud of God—
>   Strength and comfort glorious!

3   With the cloud continually a fire does flash,
      Burning us! Burning us!
    It exposes sin, the soul life, and the flesh,
      Burning us! Burning us!

> Let it burn! the jealous flame of God;
>   Let it burn continually!
> Let it burn! this all-consuming flame;
>   Let it burn us thoroughly!

4   Then from out the fire does the electrum glow,
      Shining forth! Shining forth!
    The redeeming God does our experience show,
      Shining forth! Shining forth!

> Let Him shine! This gold and silver One;
>   Let Him shine for all to see!
> 'Tis the Lamb-God who has now become
>   Our enjoyment inwardly.

5   Let the wind, cloud, fire and th' electrum be
      Wrought in us, o'er and o'er;
    Let this cycle be repeated constantly
      More and more, more and more!

> Blow and hover, burn and shine forth, Lord,
>   All our being to possess,
> That we all may gain Thee constantly
>   All Thy likeness to express.

Composition for prophecy with main point and sub-points: _____

_____

_____

_____

_____

_____

_____

_____

_____

_____

_____

_____

_____

_____

_____

_____

_____

_____

_____

_____

_____

_____

_____

_____

_____

_____

_____

_____

_____

_____

_____

_____

_____

_____

_____

_____

_____

The Universal Spreading of Christ as the True Vine—the Organism of the Triune God in the Economy of God

Scripture Reading: John 15:1-2, 4-5, 7-8, 12, 16-17

Day 1 I. **The organic increase and universal spreading of the church is the multiplication of Christ in the fruit-bearing of the branches of Christ, the true vine in the universe, as the organism of the Triune God in the economy of God (John 15:1-2, 4-5, 8, 16).**

II. **As the true vine, Christ is the center of God's operation in the universe (v. 1; Col. 1:15-18; 2:9; 3:4, 11):**

A. The entire universe is a vineyard, and centered in this vineyard is the true vine, which is Christ the Son; everything that God the Father is and has is for this center, is embodied in this center, and is expressed through this center (John 15:1; 1:18; 3:35; 16:15; 17:10).

B. The true vine—the center of God's operation in the universe—is for the propagation and multiplication of life (15:5, 8, 16):

1. To propagate life is to spread life widely, and to multiply life is to reproduce life (10:10; 12:24; 15:16).

2. This propagation and multiplication of life is to express life for the glorification of the Father (v. 8).

Day 2 C. The vine and the branches are an organism to glorify the Father, to have the intent, the content, the inner life, and the inner riches released and expressed from within (vv. 1, 4-5, 8):

1. In verse 8 the word *glorified* means to have the intent, the content, the inner life, and the inner riches released and expressed.

2. When the life of the vine is expressed through the branches in its propagation

and multiplication, the Father is glorified,
because what the Father is in the riches of
His life is expressed in the propagation and
multiplication of the vine; this is the glorification of the Father (vv. 4-5, 8).

D. As the organism of the Triune God in the economy of God, the true vine is for the multiplication and spread of the processed and consummated Triune God in millions of His chosen
ones (17:20-21; Acts 2:42, 47; 5:14; 6:7; 9:31;
16:5).

Day 3 **III. We need to be brought into a full realization
of the fact that we all are branches of the
universal vine (John 15:2, 4-5):**

A. We have become branches of the vine, members
of Christ, by the branching out of the vine; when
we believed in the Lord Jesus, He branched into
us (3:15).

B. For us to be a branch means that Christ has
become our life (Col. 3:4).

C. Christ as the vine does everything through His
believers as the branches; without Him we can
do nothing, and without us He can do nothing;
we need Him, and He needs us (John 15:4-5).

D. As branches of the vine, we need to abide in the
vine (v. 4):

   1. What we are, what we have, and what we do
   must be in the Lord and by the Lord in us
   (Phil. 4:13; 2 Tim. 2:1).

   2. If we would abide in the vine, we must first
   see the fact that we are branches in the
   vine, and then we need to maintain the fellowship between us and the Lord (John
   15:2; 1 Cor. 1:9, 30; 1 John 1:7; 4:15).

Day 4 E. Our destiny as branches of the universal vine is
to bear fruit for the glorification of the Father;
this God-appointed destiny is fulfilled by the
practice of the God-ordained way to carry out
God's New Testament economy (John 15:16).

IV. **When we abide in Christ as the universal vine, we have the church life (vv. 12, 16-17; 1 Cor. 1:2, 9, 30; 6:17; 12:27):**
   A. The branches are one with the vine and with one another (John 17:11, 21-23).
   B. The church life, the Body, is a life of loving one another; we need to love one another in the life of Christ, in the love of Christ, and in the commission of Christ (15:12, 16-17).

Day 5　　C. When we abide in Christ, we participate in the wonderful fellowship among the co-branches (vv. 4-5; 1 John 1:3-7):
   1. The inner life of all the branches is one, and this life should continually circulate through all the branches (vv. 2-3).
   2. The church life is the fellowship, the communion, the co-participation, the mutual enjoyment of Christ (1 Cor. 1:2, 9; 12:27).
   3. All the local churches should remain in this unique fellowship—the fellowship of the Body (Acts 2:42; 1 Cor. 10:16; 1 John 1:3).
   4. Because we are in this one flow, we cannot be separated by space; no matter where we may be, we are all in the one fellowship (1 Cor. 1:9).

Day 6　V. **For the universal spreading of Christ as the true vine, we need to have effective prayers for fruit-bearing (John 15:7, 16):**
   A. Prayer is man cooperating and co-working with God, allowing God to express Himself through man and thus accomplish His purpose (Rom. 8:26-27; James 5:17):
   1. A praying one will cooperate with God, work together with God, and allow God to express Himself and His desire from within him and through him.
   2. Real prayers cause our being to be wholly mingled with God, causing us to become a person of two parties—God mingled with man (1 Cor. 6:17).

B. We need to pray in the Lord's name as the issue
of our abiding in the Lord and of His words abiding in us (John 15:7, 16):

  1. When we abide in the Lord and let His words
abide in us, we actually are one with Him,
and He works within us, and there will be a
desire in us that comes out of His words, and
His desire will become our desire (v. 7):

    a. When we ask in prayer for what we will,
it is not only we who are praying, for He
is praying in our praying.

    b. The Lord will answer this kind of prayer,
because it issues from our abiding in the
Lord and from His words abiding in us.

  2. To ask in the Lord's name requires us to
abide in the Lord and allow Him and His
words to abide in us so that we may actually
be one with Him (v. 16):

    a. When we ask, He asks in our asking.

    b. This kind of asking is related to fruit-
bearing and will surely be answered by
the Father (vv. 7, 16).

Morning Nourishment

John
15:1-2

I am the true vine, and My Father is the husbandman. Every branch in Me that does not bear fruit, He takes it away; and every *branch* that bears fruit, He prunes it that it may bear more fruit.

Col.
2:9

...In Him dwells all the fullness of the Godhead bodily.

The organic increase of the church is the multiplication of Christ in the fruit-bearing by the branches of Christ, the true vine in the universe, as the organism of the Triune God (John 15:1, 5, 8). All the Christians are the duplication and the multiplication of Christ. We, as the many grains, are a multiplication of Christ, as the one grain which fell into the earth to die (12:24). This multiplication of Christ is in the fruit-bearing by the branches of Christ. As His branches, we must go forth to bear fruit. The Lord Jesus said that He appointed us to go forth to bear fruit and that our fruit should remain (15:16). The fruit borne by us is the multiplication of the vine tree.

The vine tree with all its branches and all its fruit is the organism of the Triune God. The Triune God in His organism is the focus of [John 14—16]. This organism is the increase of the church. (*The Organic Building Up of the Church as the Body of Christ to Be the Organism of the Processed and Dispensing Triune God,* p. 32)

Today's Reading

As branches of this divine organism, we have to live an increasing life, which is a fruit-bearing life. If we say that we enjoy Christ and abide in Christ, according to John 15, we must be bearing fruit. If we are not bearing fruit and we say that we are abiding in Christ, we are deceiving ourselves. Genuine abiding in Christ will cause us to bear fruit....We are branches, and the duty and responsibility of the branches is fruit-bearing. The fruit borne by the branches is the multiplication and the duplication of the vine tree. The increase of the vine tree is the increase of Christ, and the increase of Christ is the increase of the church. (*The Organic Building Up of the Church as the Body of Christ to Be the Organism of the Processed and Dispensing Triune God,* p. 32)

In John 15:1 the Lord Jesus said, "I am the true vine." It is the

Father's pleasure that all He is, all the riches of His nature, and all the fullness of the Godhead be the riches of this vine. The vine is thus the embodiment of the fullness of the riches of divinity and of the Godhead. As the vine, Christ is the center of God's operation in the universe. The entire universe is a vineyard, and centered in this vineyard is the vine, who is Christ the Son. Everything is centered in Him. God the Father is the source and the founder, and God the Son is the center. Everything that God the Father is and has is for the center, is embodied in the center, and is expressed through the center. God the Father is expressed, manifested, and glorified through the vine.

As the vine Christ is the embodiment...of the Godhead. "In Him dwells all the fullness of the Godhead bodily" (Col. 2:9).... [Moreover], according to John 1:18, He is the declaration, the manifestation, of God. Therefore, the Son of God, God's universal vine, is His embodiment and manifestation.

As the vine Christ is an organism full of life, like the tree of life. Furthermore, this vine is for the propagation and multiplication of life. To propagate life is to spread life widely, and to multiply life is to reproduce life. A vine is not noted for its blossoms or its materials; rather, it is noted for its manifestation of the riches of life. When a vine is full of ripened fruit, we see the riches of life. Christ, the true vine, is not life for people to appreciate as blossoms; neither is He life to be used as material. Rather, Christ is life to bring forth life and to reproduce life. This propagation and multiplication of life is to express life for the glorification of the Father. When the life of the vine is expressed through the branches in its propagation and multiplication, the Father is glorified, because what the Father is in the riches of His life is expressed in the propagation and multiplication of the vine. (*The Conclusion of the New Testament,* p. 520)

Further Reading: The Organic Building Up of the Church as the Body of Christ to Be the Organism of the Processed and Dispensing Triune God, ch. 2; *The Issue of Christ Being Glorified by the Father with the Divine Glory,* ch. 5

Enlightenment and inspiration: _____

_____

_____

Morning Nourishment

John   Abide in Me and I in you. As the branch cannot bear
15:4-5   fruit of itself unless it abides in the vine, so neither *can*
         you unless you abide in Me. I am the vine; you are the
         branches. He who abides in Me and I in him, he bears
         much fruit; for apart from Me you can do nothing.
   8   In this is My Father glorified, that you bear much fruit
         and *so* you will become My disciples.

The vine and the branches are an organism to glorify the
Father....[This means that] the vine and the branches are an
organism...to have the intent, the content, the inner life, and the
inner riches released and expressed from within. As an organism
to glorify the Father, the vine and the branches express the riches
of the divine life. When the vine tree bears clusters of grapes, that
is the time when the riches of the divine life are expressed. This
expression is the glorification of the Father because the Father
is the divine life. The Father is the source and the substance of
the vine tree. Without the fruit, the essence, substance, and life
of the vine tree would be concealed, hidden, and confined. However, the riches of the inner life of the vine are expressed in the
clusters of fruit. I say again that to express the inner life in this
way is to release the divine substance from within the vine. This
is the glorification of the Father. (*Life-study of John,* pp. 395-396)

Today's Reading

This vine is the embodiment and manifestation of the Godhead....In Colossians 2:9 we see the Son as the embodiment of the
Godhead, and in John 1:18 we see Him as the declaration, the
manifestation, of God. So the very Son of God, who is God's universal vine, is God's embodiment and manifestation.

The propagation and multiplication of life are to express life
for the glorification of the Father. When the life of the vine is
expressed through the branches in its propagation and multiplication, the Father is glorified, because what the Father is in the
riches of His life is expressed in the propagation and multiplication of the vine.

This organism of the vine and the branches is the expression of God the Father in the Son through His Body, the church. In this regard we need to consider Genesis 1:26. Have you ever thought that the church is found in Genesis 1:26? The church is there. The expression of the Father is also there. If you were to ask how this can be so, I would reply that the expression is the image. God created man in His own image. Eventually, man became the expression of God. Then how about the church? Please notice that the man mentioned in Genesis 1:26 is not an individual man but a corporate man. God did not create millions of men; He created a corporate man who includes millions of persons. Properly speaking, the man mentioned in Genesis 1:26 is mankind, and mankind is not individual but corporate. What is the church? The church is a selected part of mankind. We may take as an illustration of this definition of the church the example of the wood used in making furniture. Although I may collect much material for the purpose of making a table, eventually I shall select only the best part of this material to use in making the table. After the table is made, I will cast the leftovers aside....Mankind is the material that God is using to make the church....God has selected only a part of mankind to be regenerated and become the church.

The church is a corporate entity. This corporate entity was sown as a seed in Genesis 1:26 and will be reaped as a harvest in Revelation 21 where we see the New Jerusalem as the ultimate consummation of the organism that expresses the divine image....The seed is sown in Genesis, the harvest is reaped in Revelation 21, and the crop is here on earth today. (*Life-study of John,* pp. 398-399, 397)

The Divine Trinity's organism is for the multiplication and spread of the processed Triune God. This organism is to have the processed Triune God multiplied in millions of His chosen ones. (*The God-ordained Way to Practice the New Testament Economy,* p. 104)

Further Reading: Life-study of John, msg. 33; *The God-ordained Way to Practice the New Testament Economy,* ch. 11*

Enlightenment and inspiration: _____

_____

_____

_____

Morning Nourishment

John   That everyone who believes into Him may have
3:15   eternal life.
Col.   When Christ our life is manifested, then you also
3:4   will be manifested with Him in glory.
Phil.   I am able to do all things in Him who empowers
4:13   me.

Christ, the infinite God, is the vine, and we are His branches. We are actually branches of the infinite God, organically one with Him. This means that we have been organically joined to the Triune God. Now we are part of God, even as the members of our bodies are parts of us. If we are in the light, we shall see that we are members of Christ, that we are part of Him.

We have become branches of the vine, members of the Christ of God, by the branching out of the vine. By our natural life we are not branches of the vine. On the contrary, by our fallen nature we are branches of Adam and even branches of the devil....The wonderful thing is that when we believed in the Lord Jesus, He branched out into us. This branching out has made us branches of this wonderful Christ. Therefore, Christ's branching out has made us branches of Christ as the vine. Now as branches we are filled with Christ as life, for to be a branch in the vine means that Christ has become our life. (*The Conclusion of the New Testament,* pp. 2930-2931)

Today's Reading

As believers, we are branches of the vine and are good for nothing except to express the vine. All that the vine is and has is expressed through the branches. Individually, the branches are the regenerated ones. Corporately, they are the church, the Body of Christ. The branches, the believers in Christ the Son, are for the expression of the Son with the Father through fruit-bearing.

As branches of the vine, we need to abide in the vine, the Christ of God. The Lord Jesus said, "Abide in Me and I in you. As the branch cannot bear fruit of itself unless it abides in the vine, so neither can you unless you abide in Me. I am the vine; you are the branches. He who abides in Me and I in him, he bears much fruit, for apart from Me you can do nothing" (John 15:4-5). Only when the branches abide in the vine can the vine be everything to them. This is the reason the Lord said concerning Himself as the vine and us as the branches, "Abide in Me and I in you." Our life and enjoyment are to abide in the vine. Our destiny as branches is to remain in the vine.

Apart from the vine, we, the branches, can do nothing. A branch of a vine cannot live by itself, for it will wither and die apart from the vine. The relationship between the branches and the vine portrays the relationship between us and the Lord Jesus. We are nothing, we have nothing, and we can do nothing apart from Him. What we are, what we have, and what we do must be in the Lord and by the Lord in us. Therefore, it is crucial for us to abide in the Lord and for the Lord to abide in us. We should not do anything in ourselves; we should do everything by abiding in the vine. Christ as the vine is an all-inclusive portion for our daily enjoyment. Because we are branches to the Lord and the Lord is the vine to us, we must abide in Him and let Him abide in us. Then in our experience Christ will be everything to us for our enjoyment.

Abiding in the Christ of God is a crucial matter. Fruit-bearing depends on abiding. Our abiding depends on a clear vision that we are branches in the vine. If we are to abide in the vine, we must see the fact that we are branches in the vine. If we see that we are already in Christ, we shall be able to abide in Him. Therefore, we need to pray, "Lord Jesus, show me clearly that I am a branch in the vine."

Once we see the fact that we are branches in the vine, we need to maintain the fellowship between us and Christ as the vine. Any insulation will separate us from the rich supply of the vine. (*The Conclusion of the New Testament*, pp. 2931-2932)

Further Reading: The Conclusion of the New Testament, msg. 286;
 The Mending Ministry of John, ch. 3

Enlightenment and inspiration: _____

_____

_____

_____

Morning Nourishment

John   This is My commandment, that you love one another
15:12   even as I have loved you.
16-17   You did not choose Me, but I chose you, and I set you
         that you should go forth and bear fruit and *that* your
         fruit should remain, that whatever you ask the
         Father in My name, He may give you. These things I
         command you that you may love one another.

Our destiny as branches of the universal vine is to bear fruit
(John 15:2-5) for the glorification, the expression, of the Father
(v. 8). The danger of not bearing fruit is to be cut off, dried up, and
burned (vv. 2, 6). To be cut off from the vine is to lose all the life
supply and nourishment of the vine. Many Christians consider
that bearing fruit depends upon the environment and that not
bearing fruit is therefore excusable. Fruit-bearing, however, is
not a matter of our environment; it is our destiny. We have been
destined by God to bear fruit. Because many Christians have
not borne any fruit for many years, God's destiny has been
annulled in them. The best way to carry out God's destiny of
bearing fruit is to visit people by knocking on their doors. Visit-
ing people by knocking on their doors has been fully proven by
experience as the best way to bear fruit. (*The God-ordained Way
to Practice the New Testament Economy*, pp. 99-100)

Today's Reading

We have covered the first part of John 15, verses 1 through 11,
which shows the relationship between us and the Lord. The
second part, verses 12 through 17, shows our relationship with
one another. In this part of the chapter we see that the
branches should love one another to express the divine life in
fruit-bearing. These verses reveal that fruit-bearing has very
much to do with our loving one another. We must keep a right
relationship with one another in life, that is, in love by life. We
must keep our relationship in love and love one another by the
life that is in us. This life is the Lord Himself. Loving one another

is the church life, the Body life. The Body life is a life of love and a life in love. We should not love one another with a human love but in the divine life and with the divine love.

We are not branches of many separate trees; we are all branches of the same tree. So we need to maintain a good fellowship with all the other branches as well as with the tree. This is why in this chapter the Lord also tells us to love one another (vv. 12, 17). If we do not love one another, it will be very difficult to bear fruit. If we do not love one another, it means that our fellowship with the vine tree has been cut off. Therefore, there is no way for us to bear fruit. In order to bear fruit we must love one another.

The branches need to love one another in the life of the Son, in the love of the Son, and in the commission of the Son which is to bear fruit for the glorification of the Father. We need to love one another in the Lord's life, the divine life, in the Lord's love, and in His commission of fruit-bearing. Life is the source, love is the condition, and fruit-bearing is the goal. If we all live by the Lord's life as the source, in the Lord's love as the condition, and for fruit-bearing as the goal, we surely will love one another. Having different sources of life, different conditions, or different goals will separate us and prevent us from loving one another.

Christians are fond of talking about loving one another. If we love one another in our human life, that will bring in death. If we love one another in an emotional way or for our own purpose, that also will result in death. We must love one another in the life of Christ, in the love of Christ, and in the commission of Christ. We must not love one another in our natural life, with our emotions, or for our own purpose. We must love one another in the divine life, with the divine love, and for the purpose of bearing much fruit that the Father may be glorified (v. 8). (*Life-study of John*, pp. 419, 421-422)

Further Reading: Life-study of John, msgs. 34-35; *A Living of Mutual Abiding with the Lord in Spirit*, ch. 3

Enlightenment and inspiration: _____

_____

_____

_____

Morning Nourishment

1 John That which we have seen and heard we report also to
1:3   you that you also may have fellowship with us, and
        indeed our fellowship is with the Father and with His
        Son Jesus Christ.
   7   But if we walk in the light as He is in the light, we
        have fellowship with one another...
1 Cor. God is faithful, through whom you were called into
1:9   the fellowship of His Son, Jesus Christ our Lord.

The divine purpose of God the Father in cultivating the Son as the vine tree is to express the fullness of the Godhead. To be cast out as a branch from the vine tree is to be cut off from this divine purpose. Many Christians today are cut off from participation in the divine purpose. When a branch is cast out, it loses the enjoyment of the riches of Christ, misses the rich fellowship of its co-branches, is separated from the expression of God, and is cut off from the purpose of God. If you do not bear fruit, it means that you have been cut off from the enjoyment of the riches of Christ. This, however, does not mean that a person will be lost. Perhaps you are wondering what it means to be cast into the fire. It means to be dried up. Many Christians do have the sensation of being dried up....Chapter fifteen is...concerned...with the matter of the enjoyment of the riches of Christ, the participation in the wonderful fellowship among the co-branches, the expression of the divine image, and the fulfillment of God's purpose. This is the main concept of John 15. (*Life-study of John,* pp. 404-405)

Today's Reading

The life within all of us is one life. The life in you is exactly the same as the life in me. This resembles the circulation of the blood in our physical body. The blood in our body circulates through every member of our body. In like manner, the inner life of all the branches is one. This life should continually circulate through all the branches. Then all the branches will be so living and filled with the riches of life in order to bear fruit.

Although the branches are many, they are one. They are one

with the vine and with one another. All the branches together with the vine are one entity, one organism.

The branches are in an intimate relationship with the vine (John 15:13-15). The branches are not the Lord's slaves; they are His friends. Because they are the Lord's friends, the branches can know the Father's desire that He be expressed in a corporate Body. (*Life-study of John,* pp. 419-420)

The church is the fellowship, the communion, the co-participation, the mutual enjoyment, of Christ. This Christ is now the resurrection and the Spirit. If you have seen that the church life consists in this fellowship, you will not be concerned about such things as the arrangement of chairs in the meeting hall. Furthermore, you will not be distracted from Christ by doctrines or practices.

I would encourage you all to seek the experience and the enjoyment of the fellowship of God's Son. The more we enjoy the co-participation in this fellowship, the better the church life will be. We need to enjoy this fellowship both at home and in the meetings.

In the New Testament, fellowship describes both the flowing between us and the Lord and between us and one another....In 1 John we have life (1:1-2) and then fellowship [v. 3]. There is a flow, a current, vertically between us and the Father and the Son and horizontally between us and other believers. Praise the Lord that on earth today there is something called fellowship, a fellowship among the children of God and a fellowship of the children of God with the Triune God!

Since the day of Pentecost a current has been flowing horizontally among the believers. This flow crosses space and time.... This fellowship has been flowing from generation to generation, ...[and] it flows among believers throughout the globe. Because we are in this one flow, we cannot be separated by space. No matter where we may be, we are all in the flow; that is, we are all in the one fellowship. (*Life-study of 1 Corinthians,* pp. 103, 124-125)

Further Reading: Life-study of John, msg. 51; *Life-study of 1 Corinthians,* msgs. 11, 14; *Our Urgent Need—Spirit and Life,* ch. 3

Enlightenment and inspiration: _____

_____

_____

_____

Morning Nourishment

Rom.   ...The Spirit also joins in to help *us* in our weakness, for
8:26-27   we do not know for what we should pray as is fitting,
but the Spirit Himself intercedes for *us* with groanings
which cannot be uttered. But He who searches the
hearts knows what the mind of the Spirit is, because
He intercedes for the saints according to God.

If a brother or sister has really learned the secret of prayer,...
spontaneously there will be the following result: such a praying
one will certainly cooperate with God, work together with God,
and allow God to express Himself and His desire from within him
and through him, ultimately accomplishing God's purpose. This
is according to Romans 8:26 and 27, which tell us that we do not
know for what we should pray as is fitting, but the Holy Spirit
intercedes in us according to God's purpose. Actually, we do not
know how to pray. We know what people ordinarily call supplica-
tion, but we know little about the prayer which is spoken of in the
Scriptures....We do not know those prayers that touch God's
desire and are up to the standard. This is our weakness. Thank
God, in this matter of our weakness, the Spirit Himself joins in to
help us and intercede for us with groanings which cannot be
uttered. (*Lessons on Prayer,* pp. 17-18)

Today's Reading

Brothers, real prayers are the Holy Spirit within man expressing God's desire through man. In other words, real prayers are
prayers involving two parties. They are not simply man alone
praying to God, but they are the Spirit mingling with man, putting on man, and joining with man in prayer. Outwardly it is man
praying, but inwardly it is the Spirit praying. This means two parties express the same prayer at the same time. Please remember
that this alone is the prayer which is spoken of in the Scriptures.

Let us look again at Romans 8:27. There is a clause which
says, "the Spirit...intercedes...according to God." This means
that the Holy Spirit prays in us according to God; that is, God
prays in us through His Spirit. Thus, such a prayer certainly

expresses God's intention as well as God Himself.

By these illustrations we can see that real prayers will certainly cause our being to be wholly mingled with God. We will become a person of two parties, i.e., God mingled with man. When you pray it is He praying, and when He prays it is also you praying. When He prays within you, then you express the prayer outwardly. He and you are altogether one, inside and outside; He and you both pray at the same time. At that time you and God cannot be separated, being mingled as one. Consequently, you not only cooperate with God but also work together with God that God Himself and His desire may be expressed through you, thus ultimately accomplishing God's purpose. This is the real prayer which is required of us in the Bible.

Once man abides in the Lord, spontaneously he touches God's feeling and understands God's desire. In the Old Testament, Abraham was an example of this. Because he continually remained before God, God could not refrain from telling Abraham of His intention....We only need to live in the fellowship, remain in His presence, and draw near to Him. Then spontaneously we will be able to understand His temperament, His disposition, and the principles of His doings. It is as if in our spirit we catch a glimpse of the Lord's eyes and thus spontaneously touch His feeling and understand His desire.

After we have touched God's feeling and understood His intention, spontaneously we will have His desire in us. At that moment, His desire becomes our desire, and what He wants is exactly what we want....Then we pray. This is the very thing that is spoken of in John 15:7: "If you abide in Me and My words abide in you, ask whatever you will, and it shall be done for you." This "will" does not come out of the one who prays. Rather, it comes out from that which God has anointed into him. Since this desire is God's desire, when he prays, God answers. (*Lessons on Prayer,* pp. 18-19, 141-142)

Further Reading: Lessons on Prayer, chs. 1, 11

Enlightenment and inspiration: _____
_____
_____
_____

Hymns, #1163

1   He's the vine and we're the branches,
    We should e'er abide in Him,
    And let Him abide within us
    As the flow of life within.

        In the vine, in the vine,
        In the vine, in the vine,
        We would know Thee, Lord, more deeply,
        E'er abiding in the vine.

2   As we hear His instant speaking,
    He's the rich indwelling Word;
    To abide we must be faithful
    To the speaking that we've heard.

3   For 'tis here we know abiding
    In the real and deepest way;
    If we love our Lord completely,
    We would do whate'er He'd say.

4   Then His love abides within us,
    And in love abiding, we
    Know the joy of life-communion,
    Full and perfect harmony.

5   Oh, how precious this abiding,
    Oh, how intimate and sweet;
    As the fruit of life is added,
    And our joy is made complete.

Composition for prophecy with main point and sub-points: _____

_____

_____

_____

_____

_____

_____

_____

_____

_____

_____

_____

_____

_____

_____

_____

_____

_____

_____

_____

_____

_____

_____

_____

_____

_____

_____

_____

_____

_____

_____

_____

_____

_____

_____

_____

_____

_____

**Experiencing and Enjoying Christ
as the Tree of Life,
Growing Christ as the Tree of Life, and
Planting Church Trees for the Corporate
Expression of the Triune God as Life**

Scripture Reading: Gen. 2:9; John 11:25; 15:1; Eph. 4:15;
Col. 2:19; Rev. 1:11-12, 20

Day 1   I. **For the universal spreading of the church as
the testimony of Jesus, we need to experience
and enjoy Christ as the tree of life (Gen. 2:9;
Rev. 2:7):**

A. The tree of life in Genesis 2:9 signifies the Triune
God embodied in Christ as life to man in the form
of food.

B. We may experience Christ as the tree of life in our
regenerated spirit; the church, the kingdom, the
New Jerusalem, and all spiritual and heavenly
things issue from the experience of the tree of
life (John 11:25; 15:1).

C. Eating the tree of life, that is, enjoying Christ as
our life supply, should be the primary matter in
the church life (Rev. 2:7):

1. For the church life we need to eat Christ as
the tree of life (John 6:57b).

2. All the aspects of the all-inclusive Christ
revealed in the Gospel of John are the out-
come of the tree of life (1:51; 3:29a; 6:32-35;
8:12; 10:11; 14:6).

3. The content of the church life depends on
the enjoyment of Christ; the more we enjoy
Him, the richer the content will be (Eph.
3:16-19).

4. To enjoy Christ as the tree of life requires
that we love Him with the first love; to give
the Lord the first place in all things is to love
Him with the first love, the best love (Rev.
2:4; Col. 1:18).

Day 2   D. In Revelation 22:1-2 there is the river of water
of life and the tree of life:
1. Because the tree of life is in the water of life,
the way to enjoy the tree of life is to drink the
water of life (John 4:14; Isa. 12:2-6).
2. The essence of the tree of life is in the water of
life; thus, in order to enjoy Christ as the tree
of life, we must drink of the river of water of
life (John 4:14; 7:37; 1 Cor. 10:4; Rev. 22:1-2,
17d).
   E. The principle of the tree of life is dependence on
God; the experience and enjoyment of the tree of
life causes us to be dependent on God (John 15:5).
   F. The Lord wants to recover the church back to
the beginning—to the eating of the tree of life
(Gen. 2:9; Rev. 2:7; 22:14).

Day 3 II. **For the universal spreading of the church
as the testimony of Jesus, we need to grow
Christ as the tree of life within us (Col. 2:19;
John 11:25; 15:1):**
   A. Christ as the embodiment of God is our tree of
life, and this tree is growing in us (Col. 1:27; 2:9,
19; 3:4).
   B. God in Christ has sown Himself into our spirit
as the life seed to grow a tree, a miniature of the
tree of life (Mark 4:2-8, 26-29).
   C. In Genesis 2:9 the tree of life was unique, but
today the tree of life grows in all of us, causing
each one of us to be a small tree of life; as small
trees of life, we need to grow in life (1 Cor. 3:6-7;
Eph. 4:15-16; 2 Pet. 1:5-11).

Day 4 III. **For the universal spreading of the church as
the testimony of Jesus, we need to plant
"church trees" for the corporate expression of
the Triune God as life (John 5:26; 11:25; 1 John
5:11-12; Rom. 8:2; 1 Cor. 1:2; Rev. 1:11-12, 20):**
   A. In the eyes of God the universal church, the Body
of Christ, has been formed; now, after the formation of this universal church as a complete entity,

there is the need for the spreading of the church (Acts 8:1; 9:31):

1. The local churches are established, not formed; the apostle Paul could plant a church, and Apollos could water it, but it was God alone who formed it and gave it life, and it is God who gives it growth (1 Cor. 3:6-7).

2. The way to spread the church and to establish a church is to bring it to a certain locality and plant it (Rom. 16:5a; Col. 4:15).

B. Although we cannot form the church, we have the position, the right, the opportunity, and even the commission to go to the uttermost part of the earth to establish local churches (Acts 1:8; 13:1-3; Gal. 1:2; Rev. 1:11).

C. What we are doing today is simply establishing churches in different localities by planting "church trees"; this planting of church trees is the establishing of the church (1 Cor. 1:1-2; 1 Thes. 1:1).

Day 5
&
Day 6

D. The local churches as church trees are golden lampstands, which are actually living, golden trees (Rev. 1:11-12, 20):

1. The golden lampstands signify the local churches as the reproduction of Christ and the reprint of the Spirit (Exo. 25:31-40; Zech. 4:2, 6, 10; Rev. 5:6; 1:11, 20).

2. In figure, the golden lampstand signifies the church as the embodiment and the expression of the Triune God (vv. 11-12).

3. As saints in the local churches, we all are parts of a wonderful golden tree.

4. The symbol of the golden lampstand indicates that the Triune God is a living tree, growing, budding, and blossoming, and the description of the lampstand conveys the idea of growth (Exo. 25:31-32; Eph. 4:14-16):

a. The lampstand is growing through the branches and within them; this indicates

that Christ is growing in us (Col. 2:19;
John 3:29a, 30a).

b. It is crucial for all the branches to give
the lampstand a free way to grow in them
and through them (Eph. 4:15-16).

c. The more the lampstand grows in the
branches, the more it will blossom and
shine, and the more light there will be
(v. 15; 5:8-9).

5. To plant a church tree is to establish a local
church as a golden lampstand.

E. Our burden is to bring the church as a tree to
every city, town, and village and plant a church
there (Acts 8:1; 13:1; Col. 4:15-16):

1. We all need to be faithful to carry out the burden to establish local churches by planting
church trees (Rom. 16:16b; Gal. 1:2; 1 Thes.
1:1; 2:14).

2. The married couples should be like Prisca
and Aquila, who planted a church tree wherever they went; wherever they were, they
were willing to bear the burden of the practice of the church by opening up their home
(Rom. 16:3-5a; 1 Cor. 16:19).

3. If we all have the desire to establish churches
by planting church trees, the establishing of
the churches will be very fast and prevailing
(Acts 19:20).

Morning Nourishment

Gen. And out of the ground Jehovah God caused to grow
2:9 every tree that is pleasant to the sight and good for
food, as well as the tree of life in the middle of the gar-
den and the tree of the knowledge of good and evil.
Rev. He who has an ear, let him hear what the Spirit says
2:7 to the churches. To him who overcomes, to him I will
give to eat of the tree of life, which is in the Paradise of
God.

From the time that man was created, God first presented
Himself to man as the tree of life in the form of food. When we partake of food, that food becomes a part of us. This is the very intention God has toward us, that we may take Him as food so that we
can be mingled with Him to express Him in this universe. The
first mentioning of something in the Scriptures is always a gov-
erning principle, a principle which governs all the Lord's dealings
with us. The basic principle of the Lord's dealings with His people
is that they would enjoy Him as their food, their life supply.

The Gospel of John tells us that one day this very God, who in
the beginning presented Himself to man as food, was incarnated
as a man. God in the form of a man presented Himself to man
again as food, as the heavenly bread of life (6:35, 57), that man
may partake of Him. In Genesis 2 at the beginning, God presented Himself as the tree of life to man in the form of food. In
John 6 after His incarnation, He did the same thing. He presented Himself as the bread of life to man that man might partake of Him. In John 6:57 the Lord Jesus said, "He who eats Me,
he also shall live because of Me." (*The Tree of Life,* p. 33)

Today's Reading

In Genesis 2 there was the tree of life, and in Revelation 22
there will be the vine tree, the tree of life. On the one hand, the
tree of life was an item in the past. On the other hand, the tree of
life will be an item in the future. But we must also realize the good
news that the eating of the tree of life is something for today. Revelation 2:7 says, "To him who overcomes, to him I will give to eat of

the tree of life, which is in the Paradise of God." The tree of life is available in the church life today. There is a basic principle in the New Testament that what we will enjoy in the future we should enjoy in this age, and that what we enjoy in this age will be our enjoyment in the future.

In the New Testament there is the principle of the foretaste. The foretaste is a sign of the full taste to come. God has prepared the tree of life for our eternal enjoyment, but today we have to enjoy the tree of life as a foretaste. If we do not have the foretaste today, we could never have the full taste in the next age, the age of the kingdom. Undoubtedly, we will enjoy the tree of life in the New Jerusalem in the future as the full taste. But today in the church life we can enjoy the tree of life in the way of a foretaste. If we do not enjoy the Lord Jesus today as the tree of life in the way of a foretaste, we will miss the particular enjoyment of Him as the tree of life in the New Jerusalem in the coming millennial kingdom as a reward to the overcoming believers.

The Paradise of God in Revelation 2:7 refers to the New Jerusalem, of which the church is a foretaste today. Today's church life is a miniature of the Paradise of God, the New Jerusalem. The church life is a small paradise. In this paradise we enjoy Christ as the tree of life. Without eating there is no enjoyment. To eat of the tree of life, that is, to enjoy Christ as our life supply, should be the primary matter in the church life. In today's Christendom there is very little eating and very little enjoyment of Christ. In the Lord's recovery, we need to have the enjoyment of Christ every day. All day long we need to eat Jesus and drink of Jesus. While we are enjoying the foretaste of the tree of life, we are looking for the full taste to come. We are enjoying Him by eating Him as the tree of life and the bread of life. (*The Divine Economy,* pp. 28-29)

Further Reading: The Tree of Life, chs. 3-4; *The Divine Economy,* ch. 4; *The Conclusion of the New Testament,* msg. 41; *Basic Lessons on Life,* lsns. 3, 7, 13; *Truth Lessons—Level Three,* vol. 1, lsn. 1; *The Triune God to Be Life to the Tripartite Man,* chs. 1-4

Enlightenment and inspiration: _____

Are what you eat + serve what you are.

Morning Nourishment

Rev.   **And he showed me a river of water of life, bright as**
22:1-2 **crystal, proceeding out of the throne of God and of the**
           Lamb in the middle of its street. And on this side and
           on that side of the river was the tree of life...

In Revelation 22:1 and 2 there is the river of water of life and
the tree of life. These verses portray the flowing out of the Triune
God. God and the Lamb are on the throne, and the river of water
of life, a symbol of the Spirit, proceeds out of the throne. The tree of
life, signifying Christ, lives and grows in the river of water of life.
If the river does not reach us, neither will the tree of life reach us.
Since the tree of life is in the water of life, the way to enjoy the tree
is to drink the water. When we drink the water of life, we enjoy the
Triune God. Today we should not only speak of Christ and teach
Christ—we also need to drink of Christ as the life-giving Spirit.

[In Ephesians 4] Christ is the element of the Body and the
Spirit is the essence of the Body. If we have only the element without the essence, what we have will be something merely objective,
having nothing to do with us in our experience. No matter how
much we may know about Christ as the element, if we do not have
the essence, this element will not be related to us subjectively and
experientially. But when we have the Spirit as the essence, we
will also have Christ as the element. The essence of the tree of life
is in the water of life. If we would enjoy Christ as the tree of life, as
the element of life, we must drink Him as the water of life, as the
essence of life. (*Life-study of Isaiah,* p. 75)

Today's Reading

The Lord needs to bring us into the understanding of the
Scriptures in an inner and living way to see what is on His heart.
After the creation of man, God presented Himself to man as the
tree of life for man to eat. The only thing God desired man to do
was to feed on Him, to partake of Him as the tree of life....Without
eating, a person cannot exist. You may have life, but your life cannot last without your eating. In presenting Himself to man as the
tree of life, God's intention was for man to learn how to live by

depending on God, by taking God as his daily supply and as his entire supply....We live, exist, by eating. God did not command man to do anything but to eat. Man has to take care of his eating. If he eats in a right way, he will be right. If he eats in a wrong way, he will be wrong. If you eat something of life, you will have life. If you eat something of death, you will have death. The Christian life is not merely a matter of doing or working, but a matter of partaking of God as the tree of life....In John 6...[the Lord] said that He was the bread of life (v. 35) and that the one who ate Him would live because of Him (v. 57). (*The Tree of Life,* p. 56)

This simple picture of man and two trees...[indicates] that man was not created independent. Because he had to eat, he was dependent upon others. If God had created Adam with a self-sustaining, unending life, he would not have needed to eat. But man could not live by himself in an isolated way, because he was designed to need food. He was destined to be dependent.

The two trees represent two ways for man to turn to have his need met. The tree of life represents God. The other tree signifies Satan. God's supply is simple—life. Satan's supply is complicated—the knowledge of good and evil.

Notice that good does not belong to the category of life. Good pertains to knowledge, just as evil does. Both belong to Satan and issue in death. If you do not depend upon God, you are depending upon that second source. Do not think that you can depend upon knowledge or upon what is good. If you are not depending upon God, your trust is in something that has Satan as its source. However much you struggle to be independent, you are waging a losing battle against your destiny....If you depend upon God, the issue is life; if Satan, it is death. We have only God and Satan to choose between for the source of our supply. (*Life Messages,* vol. 1, p. 234)

Further Reading: Life-study of Isaiah, msg. 11; *The Tree of Life,* chs. 5-6; *Life Messages,* ch. 26; *The Divine Economy,* ch. 5; *The Triune God to Be Life to the Tripartite Man,* ch. 8; *Our Urgent Need—Spirit and Life,* ch. 2

Enlightenment and inspiration: _____

_____

_____

_____

Morning Nourishment

1 Cor. I planted, Apollos watered, but God caused the
3:6-7 growth. So then neither is he who plants anything
       nor he who waters, but God who causes the growth.
Col.   ...Holding the Head, out from whom all the Body,
2:19   being richly supplied and knit together by means of
       the joints and sinews, grows with the growth of God.

The tree of life...is a figure of God Himself as life. God is abstract and mysterious. There is no word that can fully define Him. Hence, in His wisdom He presented us a figure of Himself—a tree that grows, spreads, and produces fruit good for food. The tree of life is a figure signifying God as life to man. This tree of life is the embodiment of God as life....When the Son of God came to this earth, He came as the embodiment of the Triune God (Col. 2:9; 1:19). The Triune God is life, and this life is embodied in the tree of life, which is a figure of Christ. Thus, when Christ came, He told us that He is life (John 14:6) and that He is the vine tree (15:1), of which we can be a part (v. 5). If we put these two things together—life and the tree—we have the tree of life. Christ Himself is the tree of life.

Eating is the way for man to take this tree....God presented this tree to all mankind through the preaching of the gospel, and we accepted it. Daily we are eating Him (John 6:57) as our tree of life. Our vine tree is Christ, and Christ is the embodiment of God as life (1 John 5:11-12). Thus, the Bible says that Christ is our life (Col. 3:4a). We live by Him, we live for Him, we express Him, and we magnify Him. This is what a Christian should be. (*The Organic Union in God's Relationship with Man*, pp. 28-29)

Today's Reading

There are two main ways to grow trees. One way is to sow a seed. If we sow the seed of a peach, a peach tree will grow up. The second way is to plant the sapling of a peach tree into the earth. This sapling will grow to be a peach tree. In the Bible it is the same. First, the Bible tells us that God has sown Himself into our spirit as the life seed to grow a tree, a miniature of the tree of life. The tree of life was unique in Genesis 2:9, but today the tree of life grows in all of us, causing each of us to be a small tree of life. As small trees of life, we need to grow. We, the believers in Christ, have all been regenerated by God sowing Himself into us as the life seed. From that day a life tree came out.

Then, in 1 Corinthians 3:6 Paul said, "I planted." At times we may say that we sow Christ into people through the preaching of the gospel. At other times we can also declare that we plant Christ into people. To plant a sapling into a field is a quicker way to grow a tree than to sow a seed. Paul planted Christ....[According to verses 6 and 7], planting and watering are two steps for God to give the growth. If Paul would not plant and Apollos would not come to water, there would be no way for God to give the growth.

We need to be sowers and planters, sowing and planting Christ into many vacant sinners. Today there are many sinners who do not have Christ. They are empty, vacant, waiting for Christ to be either sown into them or planted into them. If we have some dear friends who are still not believers in Christ or are believers in Christ in name but not in reality, these kinds of friends may…feel that their living on this earth is empty and is vanity of vanities. If they would pray, "Lord Jesus, I do not want to be empty anymore. I want to take You; I want to receive You," immediately they would be filled by Christ as either a seed or a plant. Sometimes they will be blessed to receive Christ not only as a small seed, but as a large plant planted into their being. This will cause them to feel that they are filled with Christ. They will be happy and will tell others that they are no longer empty, but they now have something within them, that is, Christ. Now Christ is growing in them. Then some "Apollos" in the church will go once a week to water them. This watering plus the planting gives God an opportunity to grow in them. (*The Organic Union in God's Relationship with Man,* pp. 53-54)

Further Reading: The Organic Union in God's Relationship with Man, ch. 4; *The Tree of Life,* chs. 7, 9-11; *God's Eternal Intention and Satan's Counterplot,* chs. 2-3

Enlightenment and inspiration: _____

_____

_____

_____

Morning Nourishment

Acts ...And there occurred in that day a great persecution
8:1 against the church which was in Jerusalem; and all
were scattered throughout the regions of Judea and
Samaria, except the apostles.

9:31 So then the church throughout the whole of Judea
and Galilee and Samaria had peace, being built up;
and going on in the fear of the Lord and in the comfort of the Holy Spirit, it was multiplied.

Rom. Greet Prisca and Aquila, my fellow workers in
16:3, 5 Christ Jesus...and *greet* the church, which is in their
house....

There is an important difference between the formation of
the universal church and the establishment of the churches.
The universal church is not established; rather, it is formed
with two categories of elements: all the believers as the
extrinsic element and the all-inclusive Christ, the embodiment of the processed Triune God consummated as the all-
inclusive, compound Spirit as the intrinsic element. Instead
of being established, the universal church is formed by these
two categories of elements.

The local churches are established, not formed. Establishment is different from formation. We should not say that we
are going to a certain place to form a local church there. On
the contrary, we go to a certain city not to form a local church
but to establish a local church. The church as a whole was
altogether formed more than nineteen hundred years ago on
the day of Pentecost and in the house of Cornelius. This
means that in the eyes of God, the universal church, the Body
of Christ, has been formed. This is an accomplished fact. Now,
after the formation of this universal church as a complete
entity, there is the need for the spreading of the church. The
way to spread the church is to bring it to a certain locality and
plant it. This planting is the establishment of a local church.
(*The Conclusion of the New Testament*, pp. 2121-2122)

Today's Reading

Just as we can plant a tree but not form a tree, so we can establish a church but not form the church. A carpenter can form a stand, but he cannot form a tree. Not even the best scientist with a doctoral degree in botany can form a tree. Only God can form a tree. In like manner, only Christ could form the church. The apostle Paul could plant a local church and Apollos could water it, but it was God alone who formed it and gave it life, and it is God who gives it growth (1 Cor. 3:6-7).

The entire church as the Body of Christ, including all the Jewish and Gentile believers, has been formed once for all universally. This is an accomplished fact. What we are doing today is simply establishing churches in different localities by planting "church trees." This planting of church trees is the establishing of the churches.

No one is able to go to a place to form a local church. Assuming to do such a thing would be abominable in the sight of God, for it is presuming to do something that only God Himself can do. But although we cannot form the church, we have the position, the right, the opportunity, and even the commission to go to the uttermost parts of the earth to establish local churches.

The Lord has formed the church. Our burden is to bring the church as a tree to every city, town, and village and plant a church there. We all need to be faithful to carry out the burden to establish local churches by planting church trees. We should be burdened not just for the saving of sinners but for the establishing of churches. The married couples should be like Prisca and Aquila who planted a church tree wherever they went. If we all have the desire to establish churches by planting church trees, the establishing of the churches will be very fast and prevailing. (*The Conclusion of the New Testament,* p. 2122)

Further Reading: The Conclusion of the New Testament, msgs. 195-198

Enlightenment and inspiration: _____

_____

_____

_____

Morning Nourishment

Exo. And you shall make a lampstand of pure gold. The
25:31 lampstand *with* its base and its shaft shall be made
of beaten work; its cups, its calyxes, and its blossom buds shall be of *one piece with* it.

Rev. Saying, What you see write in a scroll and send *it* to
1:11-12 the seven churches....And I turned to see the voice
that spoke with me; and when I turned, I saw seven
golden lampstands.

As we consider the lampstand as a whole, we shall see that on
it there are twenty-five calyxes. There are three on each branch,
three holding one pair of branches each, and four on the shaft of
the lampstand, making a total of twenty-five. Since the three
calyxes which each hold one pair of branches do not have blossoms, the lampstand has a total of twenty-two blossoms. The
divine thought here is that the lampstand is actually a tree with
calyxes and blossoms.

If we have a general view of the entire lampstand, we shall
realize that it does in fact look like a tree. Furthermore, the lampstand is described in such a way as to give the idea of growth.
These verses speak of branches, buds, and almond blossoms.
Blossoming indicates growth. Thus, we must be impressed that
the lampstand is a growing tree.

As a tree, the lampstand has certain outstanding features.
First, it is a golden tree. Gold signifies the nature of God....The
golden lampstand is the expression of the Triune God. The Triune
God is a living tree, growing, budding, and blossoming. (*Life-study
of Exodus,* pp. 1081-1083)

Today's Reading

The lampstand in the tabernacle emphasizes Christ with the
seven Spirits of God for God's building (Exo. 25:31-39). The lampstand for the recovered temple emphasizes the Spirit as the seven
Spirits of Jehovah for God's building (Zech. 4:2-6, 10). In Exodus
the lampstand emphasizes Christ. In Zechariah the lampstand
emphasizes the Spirit. This is because the New Testament tells

us that the redeeming Christ has become the life-giving Spirit (1 Cor. 15:45b). As the redeeming One, He was Christ and as the life-giving One, He is the Spirit. Thus, both Christ and the Spirit are the lampstand.

The lampstand was sown as a seed in Exodus. Then the growth of this seed can be seen in Zechariah. Eventually, the harvest of the truth concerning the lampstand is in the last book of the Bible, Revelation....[There are] three categories of lampstands: the lampstand for God's building of the tabernacle and the temple; the lampstand for the rebuilding of God's temple; and the lampstands for the building of the church.

The lampstand in Zechariah signifies the need of the Spirit for the Lord's rebuilding of His temple....Eventually, the lampstands in Revelation are the reprint, the reproduction, of this Spirit-Christ.

Exodus 25 shows us, on the one hand, that the lampstand signifies Christ as the embodiment of God. Zechariah 4, on the other hand, shows us that the lampstand signifies the life-giving Spirit as the reality of Christ. God is embodied in Christ, and Christ is realized as the Spirit. Both this Christ, who is the embodiment of God, and this Spirit, who is the reality of Christ, signify the lampstand. Eventually and ultimately in the Bible, the churches are brought forth into existence, or produced, and every church is a lampstand.

We need to look at this picture. By looking at this picture we can understand that every local church is a reprint of the Spirit, who is the reality of Christ, who is the embodiment of God. God is embodied in Christ, Christ is realized as the Spirit, and the Spirit is reprinted in the church. Thus, the church is the reprint of the Spirit, who is the reality of Christ, who is the embodiment of God....The lampstands for the churches emphasize the church with Christ and with the Spirit (Rev. 1:12-13, 20). (*The Church— the Reprint of the Spirit,* pp. 27, 24, 27)

Further Reading: Life-study of Exodus, msgs. 92-93; *The Church— the Reprint of the Spirit,* chs. 1-3; *The Conclusion of the New Testament,* msgs. 219-220

Enlightenment and inspiration: _____
_____
_____
_____

Morning Nourishment

Eph. ...The Head, Christ, out from whom all the Body,
4:15-16 being joined together and being knit together
through every joint of the rich supply and *through*
the operation in the measure of each one part,
causes the growth of the Body unto the building
up of itself in love.

5:8 For you were once darkness but are now light in
the Lord; walk as children of light.

As a type of Christ, the lampstand portrays Christ as the resurrection life growing, branching, budding, and blossoming to shine the light. We have seen that the lampstand is a growing entity. Since the lampstand typifies Christ, it indicates that Christ is the One who is growing. Remember that the lampstand is not made up of only one branch and one lamp. On the contrary, as the central stalk grows, it produces three pairs of branches. Moreover, all the branches are growing and have calyxes, buds, and blossoms. As the stalk of the lampstand begins to grow, it produces the first pair of branches. Then as it continues to grow, it produces the second pair and finally the third. Eventually, the stalk itself grows to its full measure. All this indicates that Christ is growing.

Christ grows first in Himself and then also in us as the branches. Apparently it is the branches that are growing. Actually, it is the stand that is growing through the branches and within them. This indicates Christ's growth in us. We are not growing—Christ is growing in us. As the central stalk, Christ grows in Himself, by Himself, and with Himself. But in the six branches He grows in us, by us, and with us. (*Life-study of Exodus,* pp. 1097-1098)

Today's Reading

This matter of Christ growing both in Himself and in us...is a vision which applies to us in our experience with the Lord.... There are six branches on the lampstand. Man was made on the sixth day; hence, six is the number of man. This number is composed not of two plus four, but of three plus three. The number three in the Bible indicates the Triune God in resurrection. Although as

those created on the sixth day, we are the number six, we none-
theless have the Triune God in resurrection. This means that we
are created men who are now in the Triune God in resurrection.
This is the significance of the number six composed of three plus
three. As the stalk, Christ is growing in Himself and with Himself; but He is also growing in us as the six branches.

How much light there will be in our meetings depends upon
how much we have of the growth of Christ. If we have more
growth of Christ, we shall have more light. Suppose the lampstand in the Holy Place was not fully grown or had grown in an
unbalanced way. The lampstand would still shine, but it would
not shine adequately or properly. If the lampstand did not have
the opportunity to grow in full, the light in the Holy Place would
likewise not be full. For this reason, we sometimes sense that the
light in a particular church meeting is not very bright. Yes, there
is light, but there is not the full, complete shining. How much light
there can be in the church depends on the extent to which Christ
has a way to grow in us and through us. If we all give the Lord a
free course to grow within us day by day, there will be the adequate shining of the light whenever we come together. Only when
there is the full growth of Christ within us can there be the full
shining of the light.

It is crucial for all the branches to give the lampstand a free
way to grow in them and through them. The more the lampstand
grows in the branches, the more it will blossom and shine, and the
more light there will be. Then when we come together in the
church meetings, the light will gradually become brighter and
brighter. Many of us can testify of having been enlightened in the
church meetings. Certain things related to us that were covered
or hidden were exposed by the light. This light comes from the
Christ who grows not only in Himself as the central stalk, but
who also grows in us as the branches of the lampstand. (*Life-
study of Exodus*, pp. 1098, 1100-1101)

Further Reading: Life-study of Exodus, msg. 94; The Tree of Life, ch. 16

Enlightenment and inspiration: _____

_____
_____
_____

Hymns, #1259

1 See the local churches,
    'Midst the earth's dark night;
    Jesus' testimony,
    Bearing Him as light.
    Formed by Him, unmeasured,
    In the Spirit's mold—
    All are one in nature,
    One pure work of gold.

      See the local churches,
      'Midst the earth's dark night;
      Burning in the Spirit,
      Shining forth with Christ.

2 God in Christ, embodied,
    As God's lampstand, He
    Has become the Spirit,
    The reality.
    Spirit as the lampstand
    Has been multiplied;
    Many local churches,
    Now are realized!

3 Caring for the churches
    Is the Son of Man:
    Voice of many waters,
    Stars in His right hand;
    Eyes aflame; His face is
    Shining as the sun;
    Churches—fear no trial,
    He's the living One!

4 What can quench the lampstands?
    Who can them defy?
    More the opposition—
    More they multiply!
    Deeper darkness 'round them,
    Brighter do they shine.
    They are constituted
    With the life divine.

5 Soon the local churches
    Shall the Bride become,
    Bringing in that city—
    New Jerusalem.

Then the many lampstands
Shall one lampstand be;
Triune God expressing,
Universally.

Lo, from heav'n descending,
All the earth shall see
God's complete expression,
For eternity.

Composition for prophecy with main point and sub-points:

III D The local churches as church trees are golden lampstands
which are actually living, golden trees.
- I enjoyed seeing that lampstands are actually trees
The description of the lampstand is full of botanical, not
mechanical terms - Exodus 25:31-32 its cups

The Recovery of Living the Life of the Altar and the Tent

Scripture Reading: Acts 7:2; Rom. 4:12; Heb. 11:8-10; Gen. 12:1-4, 7-8; 13:3-4, 18

Day 1 I. **As believers in Christ, we are repeating the history of Abraham; the Christian life is the life that Abraham lived (Gal. 3:6-9; Rom. 4:12):**

A. For Abraham to live and walk by faith means that he had to reject himself, to set himself aside, to forget himself, and to live by Someone else (Gal. 2:20).

B. Abraham's life of faith is presently being repeated among us; the church life today is the harvest of the life and history of Abraham (Rom. 4:12).

C. An Abraham is a person who has been called out by God, who no longer lives and walks by himself, who forsakes and forgets everything he has by nature, and who takes God's presence as his road map (Gen. 12:1-4; Heb. 11:8).

Day 2 D. Abraham's faith did not originate with himself; rather, his believing in God was a reaction to the God of glory appearing to him and to the transfusion of God's element into his being (Acts 7:2; cf. John 14:21; 2 Tim. 4:8):

1. Once we have this transfusion, we will experience a spiritual infusion as God's essence infiltrates our being (Rom. 8:6, 11).

2. Faith is our reaction to God, produced by His transfusion, infusion, and saturation (Heb. 12:2; Gal. 2:20; cf. Mark 11:22).

Day 3 II. **If we would walk in the steps of Abraham's faith, we must live the life of the altar and the tent, taking Christ as our life and the church as our living (Rom. 4:12; Heb. 11:9; Gen. 12:7-8; 13:3-4, 18):**

A. An altar is for worshipping God by offering all

that we are and have to God for His purpose (8:20-21a; Psa. 43:4a; cf. John 1:14, 29; 4:24):

   1. Building an altar means that our life is for God, that God is our life, and that the meaning of our life is God (Exo. 40:6, 29; Lev. 1:3, 9; 6:8-13).

   2. Abraham first took care of the worship of God by erecting an altar, and then he took care of his living (Gen. 12:7-8).

B. Abraham's dwelling in a tent testified that he did not belong to the world but lived the life of a sojourner on earth (Heb. 11:9-10):

   1. The tent is the issue of the altar; the altar and the tent are interrelated and cannot be separated.

   2. Erecting a tent is an expression, a declaration, that we do not belong to this world, that we belong to another country (vv. 15-16).

Day 4 C. As the true descendants of Abraham (Gal. 3:7), we should be pilgrims on the earth, moving and pitching our tents as he did (Heb. 11:9, 13; 1 Pet. 2:11).

D. We should walk on the earth but not dwell here, because the Lord is our dwelling place (Psa. 90:1), and "our commonwealth exists in the heavens" (Phil. 3:20); on earth we should "wander without a home" (1 Cor. 4:11):

   1. We need to be migrating ones who spread the church life from city to city, from country to country, and from continent to continent until there are local churches everywhere on earth.

   2. The more a church gives up people for migration, the more people it gets; the more a church keeps, the more it loses.

   3. Instead of having a burden to migrate to spread the Lord's recovery, we may become set, settled, and occupied (cf. Matt. 8:20).

E. After Abraham built his first altar (Gen. 12:7),

he built a second altar between Bethel and Ai, which stand in contrast to each other (v. 8):

1. *Bethel* means "house of God," and *Ai* means "a heap of ruins."
2. In the eyes of the called ones, only Bethel, the church life, is worthwhile; everything else is a heap of ruins.

Day 5 **III. Abraham had his failures, and there was the forsaking of the altar and the tent; however, with him there was a recovery, and recovery is a matter of returning to the altar and the tent with calling on the name of the Lord (vv. 9-10; 13:3-4; Rom. 10:12-13; 12:1-2):**

A. Eventually, at Hebron Abraham's tent became a place where he had fellowship with God and where God could fellowship with him (Gen. 13:18).

B. Abraham's tent with the altar built by him was a prefigure of the Tabernacle of the Testimony with the altar built by the children of Israel (Exo. 38:21).

C. Abraham, a stranger and a sojourner, "eagerly waited for the city which has the foundations, whose Architect and Builder is God" (Heb. 11:10):

1. By living the life of the altar and the tent, Abraham testified that he was sojourning by faith, as in a foreign land (v. 9).
2. The excellent and lovely New Jerusalem is the dear expectation of God's elect and the destination, the goal, of the heavenly pilgrims (vv. 13-16).
3. Abraham's tent was a miniature of the New Jerusalem, the ultimate tent, the ultimate tabernacle of God (Gen. 9:26-27; 12:8; 13:3; 18:1; Heb. 11:9; Rev. 21:2-3).
4. As we are living in the "tent" of the church life, we are waiting for its ultimate consummation—the ultimate "Tent of Meeting," the New Jerusalem (1 Tim. 3:15; Lev. 1:1; Heb. 11:10).

Day 6

D. The overcomers live in tents, looking forward to
the New Jerusalem, the eternal tabernacle and
the ultimate Feast of Tabernacles (Rev. 21:2-3;
Lev. 23:39-43):

1. The Feast of the Passover signifies Christ as
the initiation of God's redemption judicially,
and the Feast of Tabernacles signifies Christ
as the consummation of God's full salvation
organically (John 6:4; 7:2, 37-38).

2. God ordained the Feast of Tabernacles so
that the children of Israel would remember
how their forefathers had lived in tents
(tabernacles) in their wandering in the wilderness; the word *tabernacles* implies the
thought of remembrance (Deut. 16:13-15).

3. Their coming together for this feast to worship God and enjoy the produce from the good
land is a real picture of blending (1 Cor.
12:24).

4. The Lord's table is a feast of remembrance,
just as the Feast of Tabernacles was a feast
of remembrance (Luke 22:19-20).

5. Our enjoyment of Christ today as the Feast
of Tabernacles, in our corporate coming
together for blending to enjoy the riches
of Christ as the produce of the good land,
reminds us that we are still in the wilderness and need to enter into the rest of the
New Jerusalem, which is the eternal tabernacle (Rev. 21:2-3).

Morning Nourishment

Gal. 3:7 Know then that they who are of faith, these are sons of Abraham.

Heb. 11:8-9 By faith Abraham, being called, obeyed to go out unto a place which he was to receive as an inheritance; and he went out, not knowing where he was going. By faith he dwelt as a foreigner in the land of promise as in a foreign *land*, making his home in tents with Isaac and Jacob, the fellow heirs of the same promise.

Hebrews 11:8 says that Abraham was called and that he answered this call by faith. Then, verse 9 says that he also lived in the good land by faith. As the called one of God, not only was Abraham justified by faith, but he also lived by faith. As one called by God, he should no longer live and walk by himself, but live and walk by faith. For Abraham to live and walk by faith meant that he had to reject himself, to forget himself, to set himself aside, and to live by Someone else. Whatever he had by nature had to be set aside. (*Life-study of Matthew,* p. 15)

Today we are repeating the life and history of Abraham. Once there was only one Abraham; now there are many. The church life today is the harvest of the life and history of Abraham. Abraham's life by faith is presently being repeated among us. We all are here building an altar and pitching a tent. Look at the church life: we have an altar and a real tabernacle. This is a picture of the coming New Jerusalem where we shall spend eternity with God. (*Life-study of Genesis,* p. 563)

Today's Reading

To be saved is also to take a journey, to walk along the way, and to run the race. *Pilgrim's Progress,* a very famous book written by John Bunyan, stresses the one point that salvation is a journey. To be saved is to be called and to be on a journey. People talk much about justification by faith, using Abraham as the example. But before Abraham was justified, he took a journey. His justification transpired in Genesis 15:6. Before Genesis 15, however, we have at least three chapters telling us that this justified one was on a journey.

To be saved is to be called to fulfill God's purpose. When God came in to call Abraham, it was not for the purpose that Abraham be saved from hell or filled with joy; it was for the purpose of fulfilling God's plan....We all must hear this calling.

We all must see that to be saved means to be called to fulfill God's purpose. To be saved is to be delivered out of many negative situations so that we may come into God's goal. Many Christians have been saved, but they have never come into God's goal. God's goal firstly is Christ. We are in Christ. We are in the enjoyment of Christ. This is God's good land. Secondly, God's goal is the church. Years ago I did not realize that, in a sense, the church is also the good land of Canaan. Furthermore, God's New Testament economy, the kingdom, and the Sabbath rest are all the good land to us today. Are you in the good land of Canaan? If you are, it means that you are in Christ, in the riches and the enjoyment of Christ. It also means that you are in God's new covenant dispensation and in the church life. Many of us were saved for many years before we crossed the river. We were neither in God's economy nor in the church. Moreover, we were not in God's kingdom. Some of us had the concept that the kingdom had been suspended and that the millennial kingdom would come in the future, but we never entered into the reality of the kingdom life today.

Although according to what is portrayed in Genesis 12 Abraham was dragging along, Hebrews 11:8 tells us that he obeyed God's calling by faith and went out without knowing where he was going. In His calling, God told him definitely what he had to leave, but God did not tell him clearly where he had to go. Abraham obeyed God's calling and went out by faith. This was great. On the one hand, he was dragging along; on the other hand, he took a great step by faith. His not knowing where to go caused him to trust in God and to look unto the Lord all the time. We may say that the living God was a road map to him for his traveling. (*Life-study of Genesis,* pp. 544-546)

Further Reading: Life-study of Genesis, msg. 41

Enlightenment and inspiration: _____

_____

_____

_____

Morning Nourishment

Acts And he said, Men, brothers and fathers, listen. The
7:2 God of glory appeared to our father Abraham while
       he was in Mesopotamia, before he dwelt in Haran.
Gen. And he believed Jehovah, and He accounted it to
15:6 him as righteousness.

God appeared to Abraham again and again. Many of us have
held the wrong concept...that [Abraham] was a giant in faith....As
I considered the history of Abraham, I realized that he was not
the giant of faith. The only giant of faith is God Himself. God,
as the giant of faith, transfused Himself into him. After Abraham had spent time in God's presence, he could not help believing
in Him, because he had been transfused with God. Thus, Abraham was attracted to God and reacted to Him in believing. His
reaction was his believing [in the God of glory]....The incident in
Genesis 15 was not God's first appearing to him. Several other
appearings preceded it. (*Life-study of Romans*, p. 93)

Today's Reading

The first appearing was that recorded in Acts 7. Two more
appearings are found in Genesis 12: in the first of these (vv. 1-3)
God told Abraham to leave his country, his kindred, and his
father's house; in the second one (vv. 7-8) God promised Abraham to give the land to his seed. After this, Abraham, who had little experience in believing, fell into Egypt. God's fourth appearing
to Abraham was in Genesis 13:14-17, when He told Abraham to
lift up his eyes and look in every direction at the land. Therefore,
the appearing of God in Genesis 15:1-7 was the fifth; it was nothing new to Abraham. God had appeared to Abraham repeatedly,
and Abraham had experienced the riches of God's appearing,
coming to have confidence in them. During the first four
appearings, God's element had been transfused and infused into
Abraham's being. When God appeared to Abraham, He did not
leave suddenly. He stayed with Abraham for a length of time....
[In Genesis 18] He stayed with him for about half a day, convers-
ing with him for hours as with an intimate friend. Throughout

that whole visitation Abraham was infused with God. During the fifth appearing (Gen. 15) God told Abraham that the number of his seed would be like the stars of heaven. As a result of the fifth appearing, Abraham had experienced such a rich infusion of God that he believed. "And he believed Jehovah, and He accounted it to him as righteousness" (Rom. 4:3; Gen. 15:6).

Abraham's faith did not come from his natural ability, and it did not originate with himself. His believing in God was a reaction to the heavenly radium, a response to the divine infusion. Figuratively speaking, Abraham's believing was simply God working like radium within him....Genuine faith is the working of God within us. This is why God counted Abraham's faith as righteousness. It seemed that God was saying, "This faith is something of Me. It corresponds to Me. This is Abraham's righteousness before Me." What was that righteousness? It was the righteousness of God.

God transfuses Himself into us. Once we have this transfusion, we will experience a spiritual infusion as God's essence infiltrates our being. This infusion of God's element will saturate and permeate us...with God's element.

This permeation causes a reaction. The spiritual virtues and divine attributes that have been transmitted into us will react within us. The first reaction is believing. This is our faith. This is the highest definition of faith. Faith is not our natural ability or virtue. Faith is our reaction toward God, which results from God's transfusing Himself into us and infusing His divine elements into our being. When God's elements permeate our being, we react to Him, and this reaction is faith. Faith is not a human virtue; it is absolutely a reaction caused by a divine infusion, which saturates and permeates our being. Once we have such a faith, we can never lose it. It is deeper than our blood, for it has been infused into us and constituted into our being. Although we may try not to believe, we can never succeed. This is what the Bible means by believing in God. (*Life-study of Romans*, pp. 93-94, 90-91)

Further Reading: Life-study of Romans, msg. 8

Enlightenment and inspiration: _____

_____

_____

_____

Morning Nourishment

Gen. And Jehovah appeared to Abram and said, To your
12:7 seed I will give this land. And there he built an altar
to Jehovah who had appeared to him.
13:18 And Abram moved his tent and came and dwelt by
the oaks of Mamre, which are in Hebron, and there
he built an altar to Jehovah.

After Abraham had arrived at Moreh and after God had reappeared to him, he built an altar (Gen. 12:7). This was the first altar that Abraham built. In order to live by faith, we must first of all build an altar. In the Bible an altar means that we have all for God and serve God. Building an altar means that we offer everything we are and have to God. We need to place all that we are and all that we have on the altar. Before we do anything for God, God would say to us, "Child, don't do anything for Me. I want you. I want you to put all that you are and all that you have on the altar for Me." This is real fellowship, real worship. The real worship of the called ones is to put all that we are and have on the altar.

An altar means that we do not keep anything for ourselves. An altar means that we realize that we are here on earth for God. An altar means that our life is for God, that God is our life, and that the meaning of our life is God. So we put everything on the altar. We are not here making a name for ourselves; we are putting everything on the altar for the sake of His name. (*Life-study of Genesis*, pp. 555-556)

Today's Reading

After Abraham built an altar, he pitched a tent (Gen. 12:7-8). At Babel, the people firstly built a city and then erected a tower. But Abraham firstly built an altar and then erected a tent. This means that Abraham was for God. The first thing he did was to take care of the worship of God, of his fellowship with God. Secondly, he took care of his living. The tent was for Abraham's living. Abraham did not take care of his living first. That was secondary. With Abraham, the primary matter was to consecrate everything to God, to worship and serve God, and to have fellowship with God. Only then did Abraham pitch a tent for his living. Abraham's dwelling in a tent indicated that he did not belong to the world but was a testimony to the people (Heb. 11:9). (*Life-study of Genesis,* pp. 559-560)

The life of a Christian is the life of the altar and the tent. The altar is toward God while the tent is toward the world. In His presence, God requires that His children have an altar and on the earth, that they have a tent. An altar calls for a tent, and a tent in turn demands an altar. It is impossible to have an altar without a tent, and it is also impossible to have a tent without a return to the altar. The altar and the tent are interrelated; they cannot be separated.

God appeared to Abraham, and Abraham built an altar. This altar was not for a sin offering but for a burnt offering. A sin offering is for redemption, while a burnt offering is an offering of ourselves to God....It was the kind of altar spoken of in Romans 12:1: "I exhort you therefore, brothers, through the compassions of God to present your bodies a living sacrifice, holy, well pleasing to God, which is your reasonable service."

The altar has its issue in the tent....A tent is something movable; it does not take root anywhere. Through the altar God deals with us; through the tent God deals with our possessions. At the altar Abraham offered up his all to God....Everything we have should be placed on the altar. But there is still something left. These are the things that are for our own use. However, they are not ours; they are to be left in the tent. We have to remember that anything that has not passed the altar cannot even be in the tent. But not everything that has passed the altar is consumed. Many things are burned away by the fire and are gone. When we consecrate many things to God, He takes them and nothing is left behind. But God leaves some of the things offered on the altar for our own use. The things that have passed through the altar and are for our use can only be kept in the tent. (Watchman Nee, *The Life of the Altar and the Tent,* pp. 1, 4, 7-8)

Further Reading: The Life of the Altar and the Tent; Life-study of Genesis, msg. 33; *The History of God in His Union with Man,* ch. 5

Enlightenment and inspiration: _____

_____
_____
_____

Morning Nourishment

Heb. By faith he dwelt as a foreigner in the land of promise
11:9 as in a foreign *land,* making his home in tents...
13 ...Confessing that they were strangers and sojourners on the earth.
Gen. And he proceeded from there to the mountain on the
12:8 east of Bethel and pitched his tent, with Bethel on the
west and Ai on the east; and there he built an altar to
Jehovah and called upon the name of Jehovah.

According to the Bible, Christians should be moving, not
standing. We are the true descendants of Abraham (Gal. 3:7).
We should be pilgrims on the earth, moving and pitching our
tents as he did (Heb. 11:9, 13; 1 Pet. 2:11). We should walk on the
earth but not "dwell on the earth." We have a "commonwealth...
in the heavens" (Phil. 3:20). On earth we should "wander without
a home" (1 Cor. 4:11). If we have an established dwelling place on
earth and cannot migrate, we are not up to the Christian standard; we have a problem. We are rooted on the earth. We must be
like nomads and always be moving. When we move, the gospel
moves with us. We carry the germs of the gospel with us. Wherever we go, the gospel spreads like a contagion. The gospel should
spread to all lands this way. (*The Collected Works of Watchman
Nee,* vol. 55, p. 51)

Today's Reading

In Acts 8:1 we see that persecution came against the church in
Jerusalem, thus scattering the saints and forcing them to
migrate. Acts 11:19 shows that the scattered ones preached the
gospel as they went, and some local churches were raised up.
Reports went back to the church in Jerusalem, and it sent Barna-
bas to have fellowship with them (Acts 11:22). The spreading of
the gospel and the church life in the first century began by the
migration of the saints. The going out of the apostles began from
Antioch (Acts 13:2-3).

Therefore, a good number of the saints in the local churches
should be migrating ones, first migrating from city to city, and

state to state within this country, and then migrating to other countries. For the sake of the Lord's recovery, we should not be narrow sighted and only set our eyes on the local church in the city where we reside. We need a larger view.

The more a church gives up people for migration, the more people it gets. The more a church keeps, the more it loses. Do not try to keep people. Do your best to give them for the Lord's spread. Do not be narrow sighted, thinking you will lose something. You will never lose. Even if you lose on this earth, surely you will gain in the heavens. Praise the Lord for the way of migration! (*The Speciality, Generality, and Practicality of the Church Life,* pp. 68-69)

After Abraham built an altar to the Lord at Moreh, he traveled through the land. God did not give him just one little spot; He gave him a spacious land. In his travels, Abraham came to a place that was between Bethel and Ai. Bethel was on the west and Ai was on the east. Here, between Bethel and Ai, Abraham built another altar (Gen. 12:8; 13:3-4). Bethel means the house of God, and Ai means the heap of ruins. Bethel and Ai stand in contrast one to another. What does this contrast mean? It means that in the eyes of the called ones only God's house is worthwhile. Everything else is just a heap of ruins. The principle is the same with us today. On the one hand, we have Bethel, God's house, the church life. Opposite to this is a heap of ruins. Everything that is contrary to the church life is a heap of ruins. In the eyes of God's called ones, everything other than the church life is a heap of ruins because the called ones look at the world situation from God's point of view. This point of view is absolutely different from the world's point of view. According to the worldly viewpoint, everything in the world is high, good, and wonderful, but, from the point of view of God's called ones, everything opposite to the house of God is a heap of ruins. (*Life-study of Genesis,* p. 558)

Further Reading: The Collected Works of Watchman Nee, vol. 55, pp. 50-52; *The Speciality, Generality, and Practicality of the Church Life,* ch. 7; *Life-study of Acts,* msg. 22

Enlightenment and inspiration: _____

_____

_____

_____

Morning Nourishment

Heb. **For he eagerly waited for the city which has the**
11:10 **foundations, whose Architect and Builder is God.**
 16 **But as it is, they long after a better** *country,* **that is, a**
 heavenly one. Therefore God is not ashamed of
 them, to be called their God, for He has prepared a
 city for them.

Abraham removed his tent to Hebron, which means fellowship (Gen. 13:18). His tent firstly was a testimony for God to the
world and then it became the center where he had fellowship with
God. This is strongly proved by what occurred in chapter eighteen
when God came to stay with him in the tent at Mamre in Hebron.
By Abraham's pitching a tent God had a place on earth where He
could communicate and fellowship with man. His tent brought
God from heaven to earth. All of us, God's called ones, should pitch
a tent. On the one hand, such a tent is a testimony of God to the
world; on the other hand, it is a place of fellowship with God to
bring God from heaven to earth. (*Life-study of Genesis,* p. 560)

Today's Reading

Do not think that this matter of a tent is a small thing. Later,
when Abraham's descendants were called out of Egypt and entered
into the wilderness, God commanded them to build a tent, and in
front of the tent He commanded them to build an altar (Exo. 26:1;
27:1). There, in Exodus, we see an altar with a tent, a tabernacle.
That tabernacle was God's house on earth. Abraham's tent was
also God's house on earth. In Genesis 18 we can see that God came
and stayed with Abraham in his tent. At that time, Abraham was
a priest offering sacrifices to God. His building an altar and offering sacrifices to God proved that he functioned as a priest. God's
intention is that all of His called ones should be priests. We are
priests. We do not need others to offer sacrifices for us. We must do
it ourselves. When Abraham was feasting with God in his tent, he
was the high priest, and the inner part of his tent was the Holy of
Holies. God was there. By this we can see that Abraham's tent was
a prefigure of the tabernacle built by Abraham's descendants in

the wilderness as the dwelling place for God and for the priests.... In Genesis we see a priest named Abraham who lived with God in his tent. At the side of this tent there was an altar.

Abraham's tent was a miniature of the New Jerusalem, which will be the ultimate tabernacle of God in the universe (Rev. 21:2-3). As he lived in that tent, he was living in a shadow of the New Jerusalem. While he was living there with God, he was waiting for a city, a city that eventually will be the New Jerusalem. The New Jerusalem, the eternal tabernacle, will replace that temporary tent in which Abraham lived. Abraham's tent was a seed of God's eternal dwelling place. This seed grew in the tabernacle erected by his descendants in the wilderness (Exo. 40), and its harvest will be the New Jerusalem, the tabernacle of God with man....We [also]...need to be those who live in a tent and who look forward to a better country, a country in which there will be the eternal tabernacle where God and we, we and God, will live together for eternity. Abraham's interest was altogether in a better country. Although God had told him that He would give the land to Abraham and his descendants, Abraham did not care for that. He was looking for another country and for a city with foundations. Eventually, the Bible tells us that this better country is the new heaven and the new earth and that the city with foundations is the New Jerusalem, the eternal dwelling place for God and for all His called ones.

The Bible ends with a tent. The New Jerusalem is the ultimate tent, the ultimate tabernacle, in the universe. Maybe one day Abraham will meet with God in the New Jerusalem, and God will say, "Abraham, don't you remember that day when we feasted together in your tent? Your tent was a miniature of this eternal tabernacle." Abraham's tent was a seed. The growth of that seed is in Exodus and its harvest is in Revelation 21. In principle, there is no difference between Abraham's tent and the New Jerusalem, the ultimate tent. (*Life-study of Genesis*, pp. 560-561; 562-563)

Further Reading: The God of Abraham, Isaac, and Jacob, chs. 2-3

Enlightenment and inspiration: _____

_____

_____

_____

Morning Nourishment

Lev. You shall dwell in booths seven days…so that your
23:42-43 descendants may know that I made the children of
Israel to dwell in booths when I brought them out of
the land of Egypt…

Rev. And I saw the holy city, New Jerusalem, coming
21:2-3 down out of heaven from God…And I heard a loud
voice out of the throne, saying, Behold, the tabernacle of God is with men…

John in his Gospel refers to us firstly the Feast of the Passover as the beginning of our enjoyment of Christ for the initiation of God's redemption judicially….Then he also refers to us the Feast of Taber-nacles, signifying the consummation of God's full salvation organ-ically. After the full harvest of their crops from the good land, the Jewish people observed the Feast of Tabernacles to worship God and enjoy what they had reaped (Deut. 16:13-15). Actually, their coming together was a real picture of blending. All of the people of Israel were required to go to Jerusalem three times a year for this blending. The last time was in the fall after the harvest to enjoy their produce from the harvest of the good land in their praise to God with adoration, to bless God and speak well of God.

God ordained the Feast of Tabernacles so that the children of Israel would remember how their fathers, while wandering in the wilderness, had lived in tents (Lev. 23:39-43), expecting to enter into the rest of the good land. Everyone had a tent, and God had a taber-nacle among these tents, so the Feast of Tabernacles was a remem-brance of God's story. This points to what the Lord said when He established His table. He told us to eat the bread and drink the wine in remembrance of Him (Luke 22:19-20). The Lord's table is a remembrance just as the Feast of Tabernacles was a remem-brance. (*Crystallization-study of the Gospel of John*, pp. 71-72)

Today's Reading

This feast is a reminder that today people are still in the wil-derness and need to enter into the rest of the New Jerusalem, which is the eternal tabernacle (Rev. 21:2-3). Although the New

Jerusalem will be solidly built with gold, pearls, and precious stones, it will be called a tabernacle. The New Jerusalem is the tabernacle for the remembrance of how the overcomers, before the consummation of the New Jerusalem in the kingdom age, were still living in tents; they were not settled yet. When they enter into the New Jerusalem in the new heaven and new earth, they will no longer be living in tents, but they will still call their eternal dwelling place the tabernacle in remembrance of what they experienced. When we enter into the New Jerusalem, we will have many eternal and joyful memories of what we experienced. The reality of the Feast of Tabernacles is a time of enjoyment in remembrance of how we experienced God and of how God lived with us. We lived in tents, and He lived in a tabernacle. Eventually, our Feast of Tabernacles will be the enjoyment of the New Jerusalem in the new heaven and new earth. That will be the real consummation of all the harvest of our experience of God.

The New Jerusalem is called the tabernacle, indicating that those who participate in the New Jerusalem are the real keepers of the Feast of Tabernacles for eternity with full enjoyment and satisfaction.

The word *Tabernacles* in the title of the Feast of Tabernacles implies the thought of remembrance, that is, the Israelite keepers of the Feast of Tabernacles should remember that their forefathers dwelt in tents (tabernacles) in their wandering in the wilderness.

Similarly, even the New Jerusalem is called the tabernacle of God (Rev. 21:2-3) for the remembrance of the overcomers, who dwelt also in tents, in the first stage of the New Jerusalem in the kingdom age.

The New Jerusalem will be consummated firstly to be the firstfruits in the millennial kingdom as a reward to the overcomers and then consummated lastly to be in the new heaven and new earth as the full enjoyment of God's full salvation to all the perfected believers. This will be the real Feast of Tabernacles. (*Crystallization-study of the Gospel of John*, pp. 72-74)

Further Reading: Crystallization-study of the Gospel of John, msg. 6

Enlightenment and inspiration: _____

_____

_____

_____

Hymns, #974

1   He looked for a city and lived in a tent,
    A pilgrim to glory right onward he went;
    God's promise his solace, so royal his birth,
    No wonder he sought not the glories of earth.

        City! O city fair!
        God's dwelling with man to eternity is there.

2   He looked for a city, his God should prepare;
    No mansion on earth, could he covet or share,
    For had not God told him, that royal abode
    Awaited His pilgrims on ending the road.

3   He looked for a city; if sometimes he sighed
    To be trudging the road, all earth's glory denied,
    The thought of that city changed sighing to song,
    For the road might be rough, but it could not be long.

4   He looked for a city, his goal, Lord, we share
    And know that bright city, which Thou dost prepare
    Is ever our portion, since willing to be
    Just pilgrims with Jesus, our roof a tent tree.

Composition for prophecy with main point and sub-points: _____

_____
_____
_____
_____
_____
_____
_____
_____
_____
_____
_____
_____
_____
_____
_____
_____
_____
_____
_____
_____
_____
_____
_____
_____
_____
_____
_____
_____
_____
_____
_____
_____
_____
_____
_____
_____
_____

Having Fellowship unto
the Furtherance of the Gospel and
Preaching the Gospel in the Way of Life

Scripture Reading: Phil. 1:5-6, 19-21a, 22-25, 27; 4:22; Acts
1:8; 1 Thes. 1:3, 5; 1 Cor. 15:58

Day 1   **I. God's intention is that a local church would
have fellowship unto the furtherance of the
gospel, not only for one period of time but
continually, until the day of Christ Jesus,
that is, until He comes back (Phil. 1:5-6):**

A. The Christ-experiencing and -enjoying life is a
life in the furtherance of the gospel, a gospel-
preaching life, not individualistic but corporate;
hence, there is the fellowship unto the furtherance of the gospel.

B. The more fellowship we have in the furtherance
of the gospel, the more Christ we experience and
enjoy; this kills our self, ambition, preference,
and choice.

C. The move of the preaching of the gospel must be
a matter in fellowship because it is a matter of
the Body:

1. As the branches of Christ, the true vine, we
must love one another in order to express
the divine life in fruit-bearing; no branch
of the vine bears fruit individually (John
15:1-5, 12, 17).

2. When we live by Christ, in Christ, with Christ,
and for Christ, Christ is expressed through
us as love for one another, and this mutual
love becomes a strong testimony to the people of the world that we are the disciples of
Christ (13:34-35).

3. Our preaching of the gospel is by the Body
life and in the Body life; how fruitful we are
in our preaching depends on how much of
the reality of the Body of Christ we have.

Day 2 D. Paul charged the saints to conduct themselves "in a manner worthy of the gospel of Christ" and to "stand firm in one spirit, with one soul striving together along with the faith of the gospel" (Phil. 1:27):

1. When all the members in the church are "in one spirit, with one soul," this oneness will be convincing, subduing, and attractive to others for their salvation; if there is no harmony among us, this will kill the saving Spirit.

2. The word *together* has the sense of "as one man, shoulder to shoulder in absolute cooperation" and the sense of "contending as a team of athletes do, in perfect co-operation with one another" (Wuest).

Day 3 3. The phrase *striving together* indicates that the gospel is a matter of labor and endurance; the vital groups should press on according to Paul's prayer in 1 Thessalonians 1:3 concerning the work of faith, labor of love, and endurance of hope:

   a. The work of faith is the foundation of our Christian life and service, the labor of love is the key of the fruitfulness of our work of faith, and the endurance of hope is the long life of our work of faith.

   b. The endurance of hope subdues all kinds of disappointments, discouragements, and impossibilities and overcomes all kinds of oppositions, obstacles, and frustrations (1 Cor. 15:58; 2 Thes. 3:5).

Day 4 II. **The genuine preaching of the gospel is in the way of life; the gospel is not only the preaching of the word but also a life of enjoying the supply of the Body, the bountiful supply of the Spirit of Jesus Christ, to live and magnify Christ (Phil. 1:19-21a; Acts 5:20):**

A. The preaching of the gospel is the expression of

Christ, and bearing fruit is the outworking of the inner experience of life (John 15:5; Acts 16:23-25, 30).

B. When Paul wrote to the Philippians, he was living in prison and not outwardly working; his speaking of "fruit for my work" indicates that his work was actually his living (1:22):

1. The fruit for Paul's work was Christ being lived out, magnified, ministered, and transfused into others through him.

2. Paul's living work was to minister Christ to others and to transfuse the Christ whom he magnified into them; through Paul's magnification of Christ, even some in Caesar's household were saved (4:22).

3. Paul told the Philippians that his imprisonment would also work to the advancement of the gospel (1:12, 18).

C. Paul fed his spiritual children with his own living of Christ; the best way to shepherd people is to give them a proper pattern (1 Thes. 2:1-12):

1. Paul and his co-workers were a pattern of the gospel that they spread—"you know what kind of men we were among you for your sake" (1:5b).

2. The apostle Paul stressed repeatedly their entrance toward the believers; this shows that the apostles' manner of life played a great role in infusing the gospel into the new converts (vv. 5, 9; 2:1, 11a).

Day 5   D. Acts tells us that the preachers of the gospel are the Lord's witnesses, His martyrs; this means that we testify to others at a cost, even at the sacrifice of our life (1:8):

1. To live a clean and upright life (1 Thes. 2:3-6, 10) and to love the new converts, even by giving our own souls to them (vv. 7-9, 11), are the prerequisites for infusing them with the salvation conveyed in the gospel that we preach.

2. Paul was willing to spend not only what he had but also himself, his very being, on behalf of the saints (2 Cor. 12:15).

Day 6   E. Because of Paul the churches could have the growth in life and could be filled with the enjoyment of Christ; this should also be true of us today (Phil. 1:25):

1. Because Paul lived and magnified Christ to the uttermost, he could <u>transfuse</u> Christ into the saints and minister Christ to all the churches.

2. Paul's consideration to either depart and be with Christ or remain in the flesh was not selfish but was for the saints' sake; he was absolutely occupied by the Lord and the church (vv. 23-24):

   a. It should matter to the church whether we remain in the flesh or go to be with the Lord, but this depends on our living Christ, magnifying Christ, ministering Christ, and transfusing Christ from the depths of our being into that of the saints.

   b. In the Body life there is the urgent need for the Lord to gain us to be channels of supply for the furtherance of the gospel.

Morning Nourishment

Phil. For your fellowship unto *the furtherance of* the gospel
1:5-6 from the first day until now, being confident of this
very thing, that He who has begun in you a good work
will complete it until the day of Christ Jesus.
John By this shall all men know that you are My disciples,
13:35 if you have love for one another.

In Philippians Paul speaks about the experience of Christ in a
very peculiar way....Philippians 1:5 and 6...indicate that the fellowship unto the furtherance of the gospel is a good work, a work
initiated by Christ. Christ will perform this work until the day of
Christ Jesus....From the time we are saved until the time the
Lord Jesus comes back, our Christian life should be a gospel-
preaching life. We are not here for our education, job, or family,
and we are not here to earn money or to gain a reputation or position. We are here to live a gospel-preaching life, a life that preaches
Christ....Whether I speak or remain silent, my life, my living, my
being, and my entire person are a preaching of Christ.

Our gospel-preaching life should not be individualistic; rather,
it must be corporate. This is the reason that in the preaching of the
gospel we have fellowship....The experience of Christ is not mainly
in the preaching; it is in the fellowship....As long as you have fellowship in your preaching of the gospel, you will experience Christ.

The fellowship unto the gospel kills the self, the flesh, and the
natural man. It also kills our ambition, desire, preference, and
choice. This is the reason that the fellowship in the preaching of
the gospel causes us to experience Christ. Thus, according to...
Philippians, the first way to experience Christ is in the fellowship
unto the gospel. (*The Experience of Christ*, pp. 11-14)

Today's Reading

The preaching of the gospel is...a matter of the Body. In
Philippians 1:5 the apostle Paul uses the word *fellowship,* speaking of the fellowship unto the furtherance of the gospel. If this
were a matter of individuals only, there would be no need for fellowship. The move of the preaching of the gospel must be a matter

in fellowship, because it is a matter of the Body.

John 15 tells us that all the branches bear fruit (vv. 1-5). A tree has not only one branch; it has many branches, and all the branches bear fruit in a way of fellowship. This is why later in that chapter the Lord Jesus tells us that we have to love one another (vv. 12, 17). If we love one another, the people of the world will see that we are the disciples of Christ (13:34-35). If we preach Christ yet do not have fellowship and do not love one another,...we will not be very fruitful. In order to be fruitful, we have to love one another. This is the strongest testimony to the unbelievers.

All people deep within are seeking a life and love in real mutuality. This desire for mutuality is in the human nature as something created by God. Not one human being truly wants to live by himself or herself individually. However, because of the damage done by the evil one, there is no real mutuality among humanity and in human society....When we live by Christ, in Christ, with Christ, and for Christ, we have love for one another, and this mutual love becomes a strong testimony. This is the outworking of the inner life and the power to bear fruit.

In order to be prevailing and fruitful in the preaching of the gospel, we must pay our full attention to the Body life. The more we live in the Body life and have the reality of the Body life, the more we will be fruitful. Such a life will be a strong testimony to our relatives, friends, schoolmates, and neighbors. When all these people see the kind of mutual love we have among us as Christian brothers, they will be very impressed and influenced. This will pave the way and open the door for the Holy Spirit to work in their hearts. To have the real Body life helps us to be prevailing. I believe that this is the very reason why the apostle Paul uses the word *fellowship* in Philippians 1:5. All the branches bear fruit together, one with another. Not one branch bears fruit individually. (*Preaching the Gospel in the Way of Life,* pp. 91-92)

Further Reading: The Experience of Christ, ch. 2; Preaching the Gospel in the Way of Life, ch. 8

Enlightenment and inspiration: _____

_____

_____

_____

Morning Nourishment

Phil. Only, conduct yourselves in a manner worthy of the
1:27 gospel of Christ, that whether coming and seeing you
or being absent, I may hear of the things concerning
you, that you stand firm in one spirit, with one soul
striving together *along* with the faith of the gospel.

[Philippians 1:27] tells us that we must have a kind of conduct,
a daily walk and living, that becomes the gospel of Christ....We
must have a life, a conversation, a walk, which corresponds with
our gospel....The word *strive* [in this verse] means "to labor, to
fight." We have to labor, fight, and strive together. The word
together is also very meaningful, having the sense of "as one man,
shoulder to shoulder in absolute cooperation." This requires that
we be in one spirit and with one mind. (*Preaching the Gospel in
the Way of Life,* pp. 90-91)

Today's Reading

The real preaching is a battle. We should not think that we
can bring the gospel to people so easily. The apostle Paul used
the phrase *striving together* (Phil. 1:27). This indicates that we
need patience and endurance. George Müller prayed for a certain
person to be saved, but that person was not saved [until after
Müller's death]....To bring certain persons to the Lord...requires
a real struggle. We all have to learn this lesson. We cannot do a
quick work in the preaching of the gospel. To preach the gospel is
to have a harvest, and we cannot have a harvest in a quick way.
We have to learn patience.

Our responsibility is to work and to pray. As to the result, we
must leave this matter to the Lord and to time....The proper way
to work is simply to bear responsibility. Never estimate the result.
If you estimate the result, you will be either disappointed or
proud. Learn the lesson to fellowship with the Lord, to work for
Him, and to work in Him. That is good enough.

We must learn always to be in one spirit and with one soul with
the brothers and sisters. To have one soul, to be joined in soul, and
to be like-souled are repeated several times in Philippians (1:27;

2:2, 20)....Paul told [Euodias and Syntyche] to think the same thing in the Lord (4:2).

[Philippians] tells us clearly that the preaching of the gospel is a matter of fellowship. In fellowship, the most needful thing is the harmony. You can never play good music on the piano if all the keys are not in harmony. In order to work together shoulder to shoulder there must be harmony. Someone may be an extraordinary ball player, but he is useless if he does not stay in harmony with the team; he even becomes a damage to the team.

There is the need of real harmony, especially in preaching the gospel. The more tender and delicate something is, the more it needs harmony. We especially need harmony in the things of the spirit, because the spirit is tender and delicate. The church life, the Body life, is something in the spirit. Do not think that the preaching of the gospel is merely a kind of activity to be carried out in a rough, crude way. We cannot preach in this way. Rather, preaching the gospel is a matter in the spirit. We must have the tender harmony, not only in one spirit, but also with one mind and soul.

If among us there is no harmony, no tenderness and humility, we cannot expect people to be saved. We simply kill the saving Spirit. I have seen a group of brothers who...have the harmony in tenderness and humility. Among them there is not much preaching, not even much speaking, but people are saved through them. Preaching the gospel is a matter absolutely in the spirit, not in the mentality and not in argument. Therefore, we need the harmony.

The preaching of the gospel is a lifelong matter...(1:6)....We must pray that the good work that has begun and been established among us by the Lord would keep going on and on, and that we all will learn the lessons. Not only must we preach the gospel to save others,...but we ourselves must learn the lessons. Then we will be built up together by the outreach of the gospel. (*Preaching the Gospel in the Way of Life,* pp. 96, 98-100)

Further Reading: Life-study of Philippians, msg. 8; *The Experience of Christ,* ch. 3

Enlightenment and inspiration: _____

_____

_____

_____

Morning Nourishment

1 Thes. **Remembering unceasingly your work of faith and**
1:3 **labor of love and endurance of hope in our Lord Jesus**
Christ, before our God and Father.
2 Thes. **And the Lord direct your hearts into the love of God**
3:5 **and into the endurance of Christ.**

In 1 Thessalonians 1:3...the apostle remembered the Thessalonians first in their work of faith, then in their labor of love, and finally in their endurance of hope.

There is a difference between work and labor. Paul used the word *work* first, mentioning the Thessalonian believers' work of faith; then he used the word *labor,* referring to their labor of love. Nothing exhausts us as much as being vital. If we desire to be vital, we must prepare ourselves to be exhausted. It is not adequate to be vital for just one day. To be vital requires us to labor. Every farmer knows that it is not enough merely to work. A farmer must labor. This is why we need endurance. To work does not require very much endurance, but to labor, we need endurance. (*The Training and the Practice of the Vital Groups,* p. 125)

Today's Reading

In Colossians 1:28 Paul said that he announced Christ by admonishing and teaching every man in all wisdom, that he might present every man full-grown in Christ. Then in verse 29 he said that he labored for this, struggling according to God's operation, which operated in him in power....[He continued], "For I want you to know how great a struggle I have for you..." [2:1]. In these verses Paul said that he labored by struggling. This indicates that something was opposing and working against Paul so that he needed to struggle. The word for *struggling* in 1:29 can also be translated "contending," as in wrestling. This indicates that in order to labor, we need to have a fighting, struggling spirit.

In 1 Corinthians 3:6 Paul said, "I planted, Apollos watered, but God caused the growth." To plant and to water are not merely a work but a labor. We cannot plant a seed one day and after two days expect to see it grow up. After we plant a seed, we must take care of it. After one week we may see very little growth, and after two more weeks the growth may appear to be about the same. This will exhaust us and at times even discourage us. It may cause us to think that we have planted and watered in vain. However, we need to labor by continuing to till the ground and fertilize and water the plants day by day. Paul used all these illustrations to show us what kind of work he was doing.

In 1 Corinthians 15:10 Paul said that he labored more abundantly than all the other apostles. Then...he advised us to be steadfast, immovable, always abounding in the work of the Lord, knowing that our labor is not in vain in the Lord [v. 58].

In addition to our labor of love, we also need the endurance of hope. We need to be willing to suffer opposition. We need to be a person who endures in hope of the Lord's coming. According to Luke 16:9, in the kingdom age many will welcome us into the eternal tabernacles because of our labor.

Our hope is in the coming Christ with His glory, and it is also in the reward of the coming kingdom. The endurance of hope is the long life of our work of faith. Through such an endurance we can subdue all kinds of disappointments, discouragements, and impossibilities, and we can also overcome all kinds of oppositions, obstacles, and frustrations. Such an endurance consummates in gaining sinners, feeding the believers, perfecting the saints, and building up the church, the Body of Christ, for the kingdom of God and of Christ.

Some may say that to be vital is impossible. However,...everything is possible. No one has ever overcome Christ. Christ has overcome all His opposers, including us. Since this is the case, He can overcome everyone. We should simply go out with Him. We should go out in His name to let everyone whom we visit know that we are working for Jesus Christ. This will work. (*The Training and the Practice of the Vital Groups*, pp. 125-126, 135)

Further Reading: The Training and the Practice of the Vital Groups, msg. 12

Enlightenment and inspiration: _____

_____

_____

_____

Morning Nourishment

Phil. **Now I want you to know, brothers, that the things**
1:12 concerning me have turned out rather to the advance-
ment of the gospel.
22 But if *I am* to live in the flesh, if this to me is fruit for
***my* work, then I do not know what I will choose.**

To a great extent, the word *work* has been spoiled. Many
Christians care only for a work; they do not care for Christ. But
Paul could speak of "fruit for my work" [Phil. 1:22]. Paul's use of
the word *fruit* indicates that his work was actually his living.
When Paul wrote to the Philippians, he was living in prison; he
was not working. This indicates that his living was his work.
From such a living work, fruit would come forth. The fruit of this
work was Christ lived out, magnified, and ministered to others.
The fruit of Paul's work was thus the transfusion of Christ into
others. Therefore, the fruit of work in verse 22 is the issue, the
result, of Paul's living in prison.

Paul's living work was to minister Christ to others and to
transfuse the Christ he magnified into them. As far as Paul was
concerned, to die was to gain, but to live was to carry on such a living and fruitful work. It was difficult for him to choose between
the two. This was the reason he said, "I do not know what I will
choose." If you had to choose between the gain which comes from
dying physically and the fruit which comes from a living work,
what would be your choice? I would definitely prefer to live in the
flesh in order to carry on the living work of magnifying Christ and
transfusing Him into others. (*Life-study of Philippians,* pp. 59-60)

Today's Reading

[In Philippians 1:12 Paul said], "Now I want you to know,
brothers, that the things concerning me have turned out rather to
the advancement of the gospel."...Even his being in prison was a
kind of furtherance of the gospel.

He also said,..."According to my earnest expectation and hope
that in nothing I will be put to shame, but with all boldness, as
always, even now Christ will be magnified in my body, whether

through life or through death" [v. 20]. This tells us that the genuine preaching of the gospel is not merely the preaching of the word, but a life of magnifying Christ. Then at the end of this chapter, he tells us that we must have a kind of conduct, a daily walk and living, that becomes the gospel of Christ [v. 27]....We must have a life, a conversation, a walk, which corresponds with our gospel. (*Preaching the Gospel in the Way of Life,* p. 90)

[In 1 Thessalonians] instead of emphasizing the supernatural and the miraculous, Paul takes his living as a factor for the preaching of the gospel.

[Paul] says, "For you yourselves know, brothers, our entrance toward you, that it has not been in vain" [2:1]. The apostle stresses repeatedly their entrance to the believers (1:5, 9). This shows that their manner of life played a great role in infusing the gospel into the new converts. It was not only what the apostles said, but also what they were....[The apostles] were a pattern of how to believe in the Lord and follow Him. Because many came to believe in the Lord Jesus through the apostles, a church was raised up in less than a month. This happened not mainly as a result of preaching and teaching, but through the kind of entrance the apostles had among the Thessalonians.

First Thessalonians 2:1-12 shows us how we should conduct ourselves as a pattern for new believers. In order to be a proper pattern, we need to be pure in our motives, especially concerning money....If we are not pure concerning money, if we are not sincere, honest, and faithful regarding it, we may be among those who adulterate the word of God and peddle it. Furthermore, this motive may cause us to use flattery and to have a pretext for covetousness. All these are serious matters....Instead of trying to please man, we should do our best to please God. Then other believers will have a good pattern to follow. (*Life-study of 1 Thessalonians,* pp. 95, 97, 104-105)

Further Reading: Life-study of Philippians, msg. 7; *Life-study of 1 Thessalonians,* msg. 12

Enlightenment and inspiration: _____

_____

_____

_____

Morning Nourishment

Acts   **But you shall receive power when the Holy Spirit**
1:8   **comes upon you, and you shall be My witnesses both**
       in Jerusalem and in all Judea and Samaria and unto
       the uttermost part of the earth.
2 Cor. **But I, I will most gladly spend and be utterly spent on**
12:15 **behalf of your souls....**

Matthew 24:14 says, "And this gospel of the kingdom will be
preached in the whole inhabited earth for a testimony to all the
nations, and then the end will come," [and 28:19-20 says], "Go
therefore and disciple all the nations, baptizing them into the
name of the Father and of the Son and of the Holy Spirit, teaching
them to observe all that I have commanded you. And behold, I am
with you all the days until the consummation of the age." Acts 1:8
[above]...speaks not of preachers but of witnesses.
    We Christians need to realize that preaching the gospel must
not be a move or an activity. It must be a part, an aspect, an element, of our Christian living. After we are saved, the Lord leaves
us on the earth mainly for the purpose of being His witnesses.
However, the word *witness* in Greek...is "martyr." It is not related
merely to preaching but to testifying, not only by word but by our
life and living and even the sacrifice of our life. We need to testify
the Lord Jesus to others at a cost, even at the sacrifice of our life.
    Acts tells us that the preachers of the gospel are the martyrs,
[the witnesses], of the Lord. We have to be the Lord's martyrs. The
apostle Paul told the Corinthians that he was willing to spend
and be utterly spent for them, that is, to spend whatever he had
and whatever he was (2 Cor. 12:15). This means that he was willing...to pay the price at the cost of his own life....Do not consider
that this is a work, movement, or activity. We have to consider
that this is a matter of life, an item of our Christian life. We are living here for this, and our living is our preaching. (*Preaching the
Gospel in the Way of Life,* pp. 101-102)

no sacrifice, no ministry

Today's Reading

The apostle Paul said that when he preached the gospel, he

travailed (Gal. 4:19). To travail is to bring forth, to deliver, a child. All mothers know how much they are spent in travail for their children. We have to spend, and we have to be spent. We are not only preaching the gospel;…this is our life, and this is our living.

In order to have long-lived preaching, we have to make this matter normal. Anything that is normal has a long life, but nothing miraculous can have long life. We can never live in a miraculous way. We have to live by the normal way.…Our duty and our responsibility must be normal. We are here for the preaching of the gospel, so we must have a living for the gospel. (*Preaching the Gospel in the Way of Life,* p. 104)

In 1 Thessalonians 2:8 Paul continues, "Yearning in this way over you, we were well pleased to impart to you not only the gospel of God but also our own souls, because you became beloved to us." The word yearning indicates being affectionately fond of, affectionately desirous of, like a nursing mother affectionately interested in her child whom she nourishes and cherishes. This was what the apostles did with the new believers.

The apostles not only imparted the gospel of God to the Thessalonians; they also imparted their own souls. To live a clean and upright life as portrayed in verses 3 through 6 and 10, and to love the new converts, even by giving our own souls to them, as described in verses 7 through 9 and 11, are the prerequisites for infusing others with the salvation conveyed in the gospel we preach.

Paul's word in verse 8 about imparting their own souls to the Thessalonians can be compared to his word in 2 Corinthians 12 about being spent for the sake of the believers. Paul was willing to spend not only what he had, but was willing to spend himself, his very being. The apostles were willing to impart what they were into the believers. This can be compared to a nursing mother giving herself to her child. (*Life-study of 1 Thessalonians,* pp. 102-103)

Further Reading: Life-study of 1 Thessalonians, msg. 13; Preaching the Gospel in the Way of Life, chs. 9-10; Life-study of Philippians, msg. 16

Enlightenment and inspiration: _____

_____

_____

_____

Morning Nourishment

Phil. **But I am constrained between the two, having the**
1:23-25 desire to depart and be with Christ, for *this is* far
better; but to remain in the flesh is more necessary
for your sake. And being confident of this, I know that
I will remain and continue with you all for your prog-
ress and joy of the faith.

The words *your sake* [in Philippians 1:24] mean for the sake of
the church. The apostle's consideration was not selfish, but was
for the sake of the saints. He was absolutely occupied by the Lord
with the church. Paul realized that the churches needed more of
the ministry of Christ. For their sake, he would remain in order to
minister Christ to them.

Paul was a person full of Christ. When he spoke, he spoke
Christ. When he lived, he lived with Christ. When he worked, he
worked with Christ and ministered Christ to the churches. For
the sake of the church, he was willing to remain in the flesh that
he might minister Christ to the saints.

The faith [in verse 25] refers to what the saints believe in (Jude 3;
2 Tim. 4:7); *progress,* to the growth in life; and *joy,* to the enjoyment
of Christ. Paul was willing to remain for the sake of the saints'
progress and joy of the faith. (*Life-study of Philippians*, pp. 60-61)

Today's Reading

Whether Paul was in prison or out of prison, he was a strong
factor of the saints' progress and joy [Phil. 1:15]. Because of him
the churches could have the growth in life and could be filled
with the enjoyment of Christ. This should also be true of us today.
All the elders in the local churches should be factors of the saints'
growth in life and of their enjoyment of Christ. But whether or not
the elders are such factors of progress and joy depends on whether
or not they magnify Christ by living Him. If the elders live Christ,
He will surely be magnified in them. Then the elders will become
factors to enable the saints to grow in life and enjoy the Lord.

Our physical body illustrates how members can be a means of
supply to the Body. The arm, for example, is such a means of

supply for the fingers. Apart from the arm as a means, the fingers cannot receive any supply from the head. As an important member of the Body of Christ, Paul was such a means of supply between us and the Head. If we did not have him, we would lack an important channel of supply.

In these verses we see the very crucial point that in the Body life there is the urgent need of certain ones to function as channels of supply. We need members like Paul. When such members die, the transfusion of Christ is, in a very real sense, interrupted. But as long as such ones are with us, the transfusion continues unabated, and we can boast in them in Christ. The leading ones in all the local churches should be such channels, such means of supply.

It should matter to the church whether we live or die. Our living should matter greatly to the saints. But...this...depends on the degree to which we live Christ, minister Christ, and infuse others with Christ....It should matter to the church whether we live or die. But this depends on our living Christ, magnifying Christ, ministering Christ, and transfusing Christ from the depths of our being into that of the saints. If we experience Christ and enjoy Him in this way, it will make a difference to the church whether we remain or go to be with the Lord.

We cannot boast directly in Christ as the Head. Rather, there need to be some members to function as channels through which others may enjoy Christ and grow in life. There is an urgent need for such means of supply. Even if there are only one or two in a particular country, many others will receive the supply of Christ. Because Paul was this kind of member, he chose to remain and continue with the saints for their progress and their joy in the faith so that they could boast in Christ in him [v. 26]. If the saints are to experience Christ, there is the need for someone to serve as such a channel....There is a great need for people like Paul. When Paul was alive, many could experience Christ and have the progress and joy in the faith. (*Life-study of Philippians,* pp. 61-64)

Further Reading: Life-study of Philippians, msg. 7

Enlightenment and inspiration: _____

_____
_____
_____

Hymns, #1295

1 Ours is a fellowship in the gospel
      Since we received the Lord;
   We're for the furtherance of the gospel,
      Spreading to all His Word.
   For its defense and strong confirmation
      We all partake of grace—
   He who began this work will perfect it
      Till we shall see His face.

2 May all the things that come to us daily
      Unto the gospel turn,
   That all may see we're bound for the gospel
      And of the Lord may learn.
   May we be bold and fearless in spirit,
      Speaking the Word of God,
   Do it in love and do it in power,
      While living in the Lord.

3 Lord, we're expecting that we'll be given
      Boldness with every breath.
   Christ must be magnified in our body
      Whether by life or death.
   We hope in nothing to be ashamed,
      For us to live is Christ—
   He is the Person in all our living,
      Our everything, our life.

4 May all our lives be worthy the gospel
      Whatever may betide,
   All standing fast in oneness of spirit,
      All striving side by side.
   Let us proclaim the gospel in fullness
      To satisfy the Lord:
   Christ is the life, the church His expression,
      Sound everywhere abroad.

Composition for prophecy with main point and sub-points: _____

_____

_____

_____

_____

_____

_____

_____

_____

_____

_____

_____

_____

_____

_____

_____

_____

_____

_____

_____

_____

_____

_____

_____

_____

_____

_____

_____

_____

_____

_____

_____

_____

_____

_____

_____

_____

_____

_____

**The Way Christ Fulfills His Economy,
the World Situation as the Indicator
of His Move, and the Spreading
of the Truths of the Lord's Recovery
for His Coming Back**

Scripture Reading: Zech. 1:18-21; 3:9; 4:6-7; 5:5-11; 12:1;
Acts 5:31; 17:26-27a; Matt. 24:14

Day 1 I. The book of Zechariah reveals that the all-
inclusive Christ, who is the centrality and
universality of God's move to fulfill His
economy on earth, is intimately involved with
human history and with the great human
empires, especially with the empires of Persia
(chs. 1—6) and Greece and Rome (chs. 9—14):

A. The focal point of the divine history within human
history is the two comings of Christ for the testimony of Jesus, the building of God (4:2-3; 6:12-13):

1. Zechariah prophesies concerning Christ in
His first coming as the lowly King entering
Jerusalem triumphantly (9:9), the One be-
trayed for thirty pieces of silver (11:12-13),
the smitten Shepherd (13:7; 11:7-11), and the
pierced One on the cross (12:10; 13:6).

2. Zechariah prophesies concerning Christ in
His second coming as the Messiah seen by
those who pierced Him (12:10), the One who
will return to the Mount of Olives and fight
with the nations that besiege Jerusalem
(14:3-5), and the King over all the earth in
the millennium (v. 9).

Day 2 B. The way to fulfill God's economy in the divine history is by Christ as the sevenfold intensified Spirit
in our spirit, and the building of the church will be
consummated by Christ as the sevenfold intensified Spirit of grace to be the topstone of grace (4:6-
7, 12-14; 3:9; 12:1, 10; Rev. 4:5; 5:6).

C. We must see that Babylon is characterized by the wickedness of business, or commerce, involving covetousness, deceit, and the love of money; our Christian life should be without the love of money, and our Christian work should not be a money-making trade (Zech. 5:5-11; 1 Tim. 3:3, 8; 6:5-10; Acts 11:29-30; 20:33-34; 2 Tim. 3:2-4; Heb. 13:5; 2 Cor. 2:17; 12:15; cf. 2 Kings 5:15-27):

1. Of the cargo sold by Babylon, the first item is gold and the last is the souls of men; *souls of men* refers to men who sell themselves for employment (Rev. 18:12-13; cf. 2 Pet. 2:3, 15).

2. This depicts not only the coming Babylon but also today's world; people sell their soul, their life, themselves, to their occupation, neglecting God and their eternal destiny (cf. Luke 12:13-21).

3. God's sovereignty will cause the wickedness in business, which the people of Israel learned from the Babylonians in their captivity, to go back to Babylon (the land of Shinar) (Zech. 5:10-11; Gen. 11:2, 9).

Day 3   D. Christ is the last Craftsman used by God to break the four horns; the four horns are the four kingdoms with their kings—Babylon, Medo-Persia, Greece, and the Roman Empire—also signified by the great human image with four sections in Daniel 2:31-33, the four stages of locusts in Joel 1:4, and the four beasts in Daniel 7:3-8 that damaged and destroyed the chosen people of God (Zech. 1:18-21):

1. The four craftsmen are the skills used by God to destroy these kingdoms with their kings; each of the first three kingdoms (Babylon, Medo-Persia, and Greece) was taken over in a skillful way by the kingdom that followed it (Dan. 5; 8:3-7).

2. The fourth Craftsman will be Christ as the stone cut out without hands, who will crush

the restored Roman Empire and thereby crush the great human image as the totality of human government at His coming back (2:31-35, 44-45).

3. This crushing stone is the corporate Christ, Christ with His overcomers, who are His dispensational instrument to end this age (Joel 3:11; Zech. 14:5; Rev. 12:1-2, 5; 19:11-21).

4. After coming to defeat Antichrist and to crush the aggregate of human government, the corporate Christ—Christ with His overcoming bride—will become a great mountain to fill the whole earth, making the whole earth God's kingdom; this kingdom will consummate in the New Jerusalem—the ultimate and consummate step of the divine history (20:4, 6; 21:10).

5. Thus, the great human image will be replaced with the eternal kingdom of God, the corporate Christ in the image of God for the glory of God.

Day 4 II. **The world situation is the indicator of the Lord's move on earth (Acts 5:31; 17:26-27a):**

A. The mystery of lawlessness is working today among the nations and in human society; this lawlessness will culminate in the man of lawlessness, Antichrist (2 Thes. 2:3-10):

1. Antichrist will be the power of Satan, the embodiment of Satan; he will persecute and destroy the people of God—both the God-fearing Jews and the Christ-believing Christians (Dan. 8:24; Rev. 12:17; 13:7).

2. Antichrist will demolish and desolate the temple of God and the city of God; he will cast truth down to the ground (Dan. 9:27; 8:12).

3. Antichrist will have sharp insight to perceive things and will speak things against the Most High (7:8, 20, 25).

    4. Antichrist will wear out the saints of the Most High (v. 25).

    5. Satan and Antichrist want the souls of men to be the instruments for their activities in the last age (Rev. 18:11-13; 2 Tim. 3:5; cf. Zech. 12:1).

B. The ten kings typified by the ten toes of the great image in Daniel 2 will be under Antichrist, who will be the last Caesar of the revived Roman Empire; all of this will transpire in Europe (Rev. 17:10-14):

    1. Before the crushing of Antichrist and the totality of human government transpires, the Lord's recovery must spread to Europe and be rooted there.

    2. The United States, Europe, and the Far East are the three influential factors of the present situation of the world; the recovery has taken root in the United States and the Far East, but there is a void in Europe.

    3. Europe, in the consummation of the fulfillment of the vision concerning the great human image in Daniel 2, is more vitally crucial than any other country or race—the crushing of the two feet of the great human image being the crushing of the entire human government.

Day 5 III. The spreading of the truths of the Lord's recovery will be a preparation for the Lord's coming back to bring the recovery and restoration not only to Israel but also to the entire creation (Matt. 24:14; 28:19; 19:28; Isa. 11:9):

A. Immediately after Christ's ascension, these four things—the gospel, war, famine, and death— began to run like riders on four horses, and they will continue until Christ comes back (Rev. 6:1-8):

    1. The spreading, running, and racing of the gospel of the kingdom throughout the whole inhabited earth is the kernel of the divine history within human history (Matt. 24:14).

2. The gospel of the kingdom, signified by the white horse of the first seal in Revelation 6:1-2, will be preached in the whole earth for a testimony to all the nations before the end of this age, the time of the great tribulation.

B. We are not preaching a partial gospel but the full gospel that encompasses everything from Matthew through Revelation—the gospel of God's eternal economy to dispense Himself in Christ as the Spirit into His chosen ones through His judicial redemption and by His organic salvation for the building up of His Body in the local churches to consummate the New Jerusalem as His bride, His wife, for His eternal expression (1 Tim. 1:3-4; Rom. 1:1; 5:10; Rev. 1:10-11; 21:2-3, 9-11; 22:1-2).

Day 6   C. Actually, the gospel includes all the divine truths; the entire New Testament is the gospel, and the New Testament as the gospel is typified by the Old Testament; thus, we may say that the gospel includes the entire Bible.

D. God's unique purpose in this age is to have the gospel preached so that the church as the Body of Christ might be built up to consummate the New Jerusalem (Eph. 3:8-11).

E. The overcomers who preach the gospel of the glory of Christ become the riders of the white horse (Rev. 19:11, 13-14; cf. Rom. 10:15).

F. May the Lord burden us to learn the divine truths of the gospel and to spread them everywhere for His recovery to bring in His restoration (Isa. 11:9).

Morning Nourishment

Zech. ...Now <u>your King</u> comes to you. He is righteous and

9:9   bears salvation, <u>lowly and riding upon a donkey</u>...

13:1   **In that day there will be an opened fountain for the house of David and for the inhabitants of Jerusalem, for sin and for impurity.**

14:9   **And Jehovah will be King over all the earth...**

In this universe there are <u>two histories</u>: the history of man, the human history, and the history of God, the divine history. We may liken the <u>history of man to the shell of a walnut</u> and <u>the history</u> of <u>God to the kernel</u> within the shell. In the Minor Prophets the "shell" is clearly defined, and the "kernel" is revealed in some detail. Unfortunately, however, most readers of the Bible pay attention only to the shell and not to the kernel.

In Daniel 2 [the history of man] is signified by a <u>great human image, with the four sections of this</u> image corresponding respectively to the Babylonian Empire, the Medo-Persian Empire, the Grecian Empire, and the Roman Empire. Although it is easy for us to see the shell, which is something <u>outward and physical</u>, we must have a kind of <u>intrinsic insight</u> in order to see the kernel within the shell, to know the divine history within the human history. (*Life-study of the Minor Prophets,* pp. 99-100)

Today's Reading

According to His economy, God wants to work Himself into man to be one with man, to be man's life, life supply, and everything, and to have man as His expression. God's intention in His economy is thus to have a corporate entity, composed of God and man, to be His expression for eternity. This divine history began with the eternal God and His economy.

The divine history continued with the <u>incarnation and</u> human living of Christ....At the end of His life and ministry on earth, the Lord Jesus went willingly to the cross. <u>His crucifixion</u> was a vicarious death, an all-inclusive death which terminated the old creation and solved all problems. His death ushered Him into <u>resurrection</u>.

Through Christ's resurrection millions were...regenerated by

God (1 Pet. 1:3) to be sons of God and to be members of the Body of Christ, the church. The Christ who was incarnated, crucified, and resurrected, the Christ who ascended to the heavens and then descended as the Spirit, has produced the church as the corporate expression of the Triune God. The church today is the enlargement of the manifestation of Christ. Thus, the church also is part of the divine history, the intrinsic history of the divine mystery within the outward, human history. This part of God's history has lasted for more than nineteen hundred years, and it is still going on.

At the end of this part of the divine history, Christ will come back, descending with His overcomers as His army (Joel 3:11) to defeat Antichrist and his army....Following this, the thousand-year kingdom will come. Eventually, this kingdom will consummate in the New Jerusalem in the new heaven and new earth. The New Jerusalem will be the ultimate, the consummate, step of God's history. (*Life-study of the Minor Prophets,* pp. 100-101)

The last six chapters of Zechariah are divided into two groups: chapters nine through eleven, which speak of Christ's lowly first coming, and chapters twelve through fourteen, which speak of Christ's victorious second coming.

In His first coming, Christ came as a lowly King and was temporarily welcomed as the King into Jerusalem in a lowly form [9:9]....Christ came also as a Shepherd (11:7-11), shepherding in Favor (grace) and Bonds (binding). However, He, the proper Shepherd of Israel, was detested, attacked, rejected, and sold for thirty pieces of silver (vv. 12-13). The children of Israel were thus left to false, useless, and worthless shepherds—the elders, the priests, and the scribes—who would not take care of them (v. 17).

In chapters twelve through fourteen, we see Christ in His second coming. In His coming back, He will be the King not only over Israel but also over all the peoples on earth. "Jehovah will be King over all the earth..." (14:9). (*Life-study of Zechariah,* p. 95)

Further Reading: Life-study of the Minor Prophets, msg. 15; *Life-study of Zechariah,* msg. 14

Enlightenment and inspiration: _____

_____
_____
_____

Morning Nourishment

Zech. For here is the stone that I have set before Joshua—
3:9 upon <u>one stone are seven eyes</u>. I will engrave its
engraving, declares Jehovah of hosts, and I will remove the iniquity of that land in one day.

1 Tim. ...The love of money is a root of all evils, *because*
6:10 *of* which some...have been led away from the faith
and pierced themselves through with many pains.
6 But godliness with contentment is great gain.

Our regenerated human spirit matches Christ, who is the
Spirit (2 Cor. 3:17)....[In Zechariah 3:9 the] stone which has been
engraved with God's engraving to take away the sin of God's people is Christ. The seven eyes of the stone are "the eyes of Jehovah
running to and fro on the whole earth" (4:10). In order to understand the significance of the seven eyes, we need to consider Revelation 5:6: "I saw...<u>a Lamb standing as having just</u> been slain,
<u>having seven horns and seven eyes, which are the seven Spirits of</u>
<u>God sent forth into all the earth.</u>" The Lamb here, who is the stone
in Zechariah 3:9, is Christ, and the seven eyes are the sevenfold
intensified Spirit. Thus, the Christ who has been engraved by
God to take away our sin bears the sevenfold intensified Spirit.
Actually, He, <u>the last Adam, has become a life-giving</u> Spirit (1 Cor.
15:45b), <u>even the sevenfold intensified</u> Spirit. Christ today is the
Spirit, and we have a spirit particularly formed by God to match
Christ. (*Life-study of Zechariah*, p. 93)

Today's Reading

[Zechariah 5:5-11 describes] the vision of the ephah vessel,
which is the measuring vessel, a container able to hold <u>one ephah,</u>
<u>used for purchasing and selling in business.</u>

"...This is the ephah vessel that goes forth; and he said, This is
their appearance in all the land" (vv. 5-6). A large percentage of the
world's population is engaged in business or commerce,...[and] in
all the land commerce seems to have a proper appearance. But as
we will see, actually today's commerce is <u>totally wicked.</u>

"This is a woman sitting within the ephah vessel. Then he

said, This is Wickedness" (vv. 7b-8a). This reveals that the woman sitting within the ephah vessel signifies the wickedness contained in commerce, such as covetousness, deceit, and the love of mammon. The seller loves money and tries to get money out of the buyer's pocket; the buyer also loves money and tries to obtain the things he wants at a low price, thereby saving money.

The vision in Zechariah 5 corresponds to that of Babylon the Great in Revelation 18....In the sight of God the wickedness contained in commerce is a kind of idolatry and fornication. Business is an adulterous woman desirous of making money.

In Zechariah 5:7 and 8 we see that a lead cover, a lead weight, is thrown over the opening of the ephah vessel. This signifies the restriction of the wickedness in commerce by God's sovereignty. Wickedness is hidden and concealed in international trade. If commerce, especially international trade, could be restricted, the whole earth would be holy.

"Then I lifted up my eyes and I looked, and there were two women going forth" (v. 9a). The one woman becoming two women signifies the double effect of commerce once it becomes free of the restriction.

The two women had wings like the wings of a stork, and the wind was in their wings. They lifted up the ephah vessel between the earth and the heavens (v. 9b). All this signifies the rapid spreading of the wicked commerce.

"I said to the angel who spoke with me, Where are they taking the ephah vessel? And he said to me, To build a house for her in the land of Shinar; and when it is prepared, she will be set there in her own place" (vv. 10-11). This signifies that God's sovereignty will cause the wickedness in business, which the people of Israel learned of the Babylonians in their captivity, to go back to Babylon (the land of Shinar). Let this wickedness return to Babylon. All the people among God's elect should be honest and simple in their living. (*Life-study of Zechariah,* pp. 35-37)

Further Reading: Life-study of Zechariah, msgs. 6, 15

Enlightenment and inspiration: _____

_____

_____

_____

Morning Nourishment

Dan. **...A stone was cut out without hands, and it struck**
2:34-35 **the image at its feet of iron and clay and crushed**
them. Then the iron, the clay, the bronze, the silver,
and the gold were crushed all at once, and they
became like chaff from the summer threshing floors;
and the wind carried them away so that no trace of
them was found. And the stone that struck the image
became a great mountain and filled the whole earth.

Let us...consider the Christ who is unveiled in the book of
Zechariah. In the first part of this book (chs. 1—6), there are five
visions concerning Christ, and in the last part (chs. 9—14), many
details concerning Christ.

In the second vision (1:20-21) Christ is the last Craftsman
used by God to break the four horns—Babylon, Persia, Greece,
and the Roman Empire—which damaged and destroyed the chosen people of God (vv. 18-19). Christ will be the unique One not
only to break the four horns but also to smash the entire human
government from the toes to the head, as signified by the great
human image in Daniel 2. (*Life-study of Zechariah*, p. 94)

Today's Reading

"Then Jehovah showed me four craftsmen....These have come
to terrify them, to cast down the horns of the nations who have
lifted up the horn against the land of Judah to scatter it" (Zech.
1:20-21). These four craftsmen are the skills...used by God to
destroy the four kingdoms, with their kings, that destroyed the
nation of Israel. Christ is the One among the craftsmen who will
come as the stone cut out without hands to smash the great image.

Each of the first three kingdoms—Babylon, Medo-Persia, and
Greece—was taken over in a skillful way by the kingdom which
followed it. Babylon was defeated in one night [by]...Darius the
Mede....How skillful was Darius! Then, as Daniel 8 reveals, the
goat from Macedonia (the Grecian Empire under Alexander the
Great) came to trample the ram of Persia. History tells us that
Alexander the Great was very skillful....Later the Roman Empire

came in to deal with Greece. These four empires are the central factors of human history. Eventually, the restored Roman Empire will be smashed into powder by Christ as the top Craftsman.

Christ's judgment over the earth will be upon three categories of negative things. First, He will judge stealing (Zech. 5:3b, 4b). Stealing signifies sins toward man, which are the issue of greed and covetousness. Second, Christ will judge the matter of swearing falsely by Jehovah's name (vv. 3c, 4c),...[signifying] sins toward God, which are the issue of a wrong relationship with God. ...Third, Christ will judge the entire human government signified by the great human image in Daniel 2. He, the last Craftsman, will come as the stone cut out without hands and smash this great image from the toes to the head. Thus, He will clear away from the earth all stealing, all false swearing by Jehovah's name, and all of human government.

Christ's judgment is related to us today. We should be careful not to steal from others in any way, and we should also be careful to be honest and faithful with God....Finally, we need to see that Christ will come as the stone cut out without hands and will smash the entire human government and thereby bring in the eternal kingdom of God. (*Life-study of Zechariah,* pp. 11, 96-97)

At the end of this...[age], Christ will come back, descending with His overcomers as His army (Joel 3:11) to defeat Antichrist and his army. There will be the meeting of two figures—Antichrist, a figure in the outward, human history, and Christ with His overcomers, the Figure in the intrinsic, divine history. The Figure in the divine history will defeat the figure in the human history and then cast him into the lake of fire (Rev. 19:20). Following this, the thousand-year kingdom will come. Eventually, this kingdom will consummate in the New Jerusalem in the new heaven and new earth...[as] the ultimate, the consummate, step of God's history. (*Life-study of the Minor Prophets,* p. 101)

Further Reading: Life-study of Zechariah, msgs. 2, 9; *Life-study of the Minor Prophets,* msg. 13

Enlightenment and inspiration: _____

_____

_____

_____

Morning Nourishment

Acts And He made from one every nation of men to dwell
17:26-27 on all the face of the earth, determining beforehand
their appointed seasons and the boundaries of their
dwelling, that they might seek God, if perhaps they
might grope for Him and find *Him*...
Rev. These will make war with the Lamb, and the Lamb
17:14 will overcome them, for He is Lord of lords and King
of kings...

Second Thessalonians 2:7 says, "For it is the mystery of law-lessness that is now operating, but only until the one now restraining goes out of the way." We all know that both Christ and the church are mysteries. But here Paul speaks of another mystery—the mystery of lawlessness. Antichrist will also be a mystery. According to Paul's concept, this mystery of lawlessness is already operating. However, there is someone who restrains it. It is difficult to say who is restraining this lawlessness. Neverthe-less, there is some force, some strength, restraining lawlessness.

Because God's purpose has not been fulfilled, that is, because the bride has not yet been prepared, God exercises His control over lawlessness. Eventually, at the time of the last three and a half years, this restraint will be removed, and it will seem that God has said, "Let the world go." At that time, Antichrist, the law-less one, will be fully manifested, and the entire earth will be filled with lawlessness....I hope that the young people in particular will be enlightened by all these points and say, "Praise the Lord that I am clear concerning the tide of the world. I know what is coming." (*Life-study of Revelation,* pp. 496-497)

Today's Reading

Daniel 8:24 says, "And his power will be mighty, but not by his own power." Antichrist's power will be the power of Satan...."And the dragon gave him his power and his throne and great authority" [Rev. 13:2]. In a sense, Antichrist will be the embodiment of Satan. ...Antichrist will also "destroy mighty men and the holy people" (Dan. 8:24), the people of God. (*Life-study of Revelation,* pp. 478-479)

Europe, in the consummation of the fulfillment of the vision concerning the great human image in Daniel 2, is...more vitally crucial than any other country and race—the crushing of the two feet of the great human image will be the crushing of the entire human government (vv. 34-35)....The periods of history signified by the head, the breast and the arms, the belly and the thighs, and the legs have been fulfilled. But the ten toes have not been fulfilled. According to Revelation 17:12, ten kings will be raised up before the great tribulation in the revived Roman Empire. They will be one with Antichrist in opposing God and persecuting His people—the Jews and the believers. These ten kings are likened to the ten toes of the great image...(Dan. 2:42).

When the Lord comes to crush human government, He will crush the feet with the ten toes. This will be the crushing of the entire image from the head to the feet. [In Daniel 2:34-35] ...Christ is the great stone who will crush the two feet of the great image, which will be the crushing of the entire human image, the entire human government.

We need to see this as a basis to understand the Lord's mind. Before this crushing transpires, the Lord's recovery must spread to Europe and be rooted there. The spreading of the truths of the Lord's recovery will be a preparation for the Lord's coming back to bring the recovery and restoration not only to Israel but also to the entire creation.

Of the three influential factors in today's world, the Far East and the United States have been occupied and taken by the Lord's recovery. Europe still remains as a region in which the Lord's recovery needs to be rooted and grow. I hope that we would bring this fellowship to the Lord and pray. We should tell the Lord, "Lord, these days are the consummation of the age. Lord, in these days rekindle my love toward You." (*The World Situation and the Direction of the Lord's Move*, pp. 18-19)

Further Reading: Life-study of Revelation, msgs. 40-43; *The World Situation and the Direction of the Lord's Move*, ch. 1

Enlightenment and inspiration: _____

_____

_____

_____

Morning Nourishment

Rev. **And I saw when the Lamb opened one of the seven**
6:1-2 **seals...And I saw, and behold, a white horse, and he**
who sits on it had a bow; and a crown was given to
him, and he went forth conquering and to conquer.
Matt. **And this gospel of the kingdom will be preached in**
24:14 **the whole inhabited earth for a testimony to all the**
nations, and then the end will come.

The first four seals [in Revelation 6] comprise four horses with
their riders in a four-horse race. All four riders are not real persons
but personified things. It is evident that the rider of the second horse,
the red horse, is war (v. 4); the rider of the third horse, the black
horse, is famine (v. 5); and the rider of the fourth horse, the pale horse,
is death (v. 8). According to historical facts, the rider of the first
horse, the white horse, must be the gospel, not, as some interpret,
Christ or Antichrist. Immediately after Christ's ascension, these
four things—the gospel, war, famine, and death—began to run like
riders on four horses and will continue until Christ comes back....
The gospel has been spreading throughout all these twenty centuries. War has also been proceeding simultaneously. War always
causes famine, and famine issues in death. All these will continue
until the end of this age. (*Life-study of Revelation*, pp. 233-234)

Today's Reading

The record of history in the Word carries out God's economy.
After Christ's ascension and before His coming back, there is a
history of the world. This history is summarized in a race of four
horses. As we have seen, the rider on the first horse is gospel
preaching. God's economy is for nothing except the gospel preaching that will fulfill His eternal purpose. Where does the preaching
of the gospel come from? It comes from Christ's incarnation, cruci-
fixion, resurrection, and ascension. These four items are the
source of the gospel. The history of the past twenty centuries has
been for gospel preaching. This is God's wisdom. Gospel preaching takes the lead in the four-horse race. What is our generation
for? It is for gospel preaching. And gospel preaching is for the

carrying out of God's economy. How can the church be produced? Only through gospel preaching. How can the New Jerusalem come into being? Only through gospel preaching.

Three negative things—war, famine, and death—help to advance the preaching of the gospel. A runner in a race does not run as fast alone as he does when others are running with him. War, famine, and death are terrible things, but they speed the preaching of the gospel.

God's wisdom is to make this age, the age from the ascension of Christ to His coming back, an age of gospel preaching. Everything on earth today is for the preaching of the gospel. Factories, printing, airplanes, radio, television, and even nuclear weapons are for the preaching of the gospel. This is the gospel-preaching age. The history of the world since the ascension of Christ is a history of gospel preaching. What are we doing today? We are preaching the gospel. And we are not preaching a partial gospel but a whole, complete gospel, a full gospel….The full gospel encompasses everything from Matthew through Revelation. In these days we are preaching the full gospel, the gospel that includes the church today, the kingdom in the coming age, and the New Jerusalem in eternity. Whatever happens today, including the opposition against us, is a help to preaching the gospel. This is the vision of the first four seals….We must have an overall vision to see the significance of the first four seals. Instead of having the view of a frog in a well, we should have a bird's-eye view. The rider on the first horse is…the gospel of the glory of Christ. This is the crucial factor of this age, and the three other horses are helping this one horse to run the race. We are not with the riders on the last three horses; we are with the rider on the first horse. We have a bow without an arrow, for we are preaching the gospel of peace, a gospel in which the victory has been won in a peaceful way. Hallelujah, this glorious preaching of the gospel is riding on throughout the earth. (*Life-study of Revelation,* pp. 238-240)

Further Reading: Life-study of Revelation, msg. 19; *The Prophecy of the Four "Sevens" in the Bible,* ch. 2

Enlightenment and inspiration: _____

_____

_____

_____

Morning Nourishment

Eph.   To me, less than the least of all saints, was this grace
3:8-9   given to announce to the Gentiles the unsearchable
riches of Christ as the gospel and to enlighten all *that*
they may see what the economy of the mystery is,
which throughout the ages has been hidden in God,
who created all things.

[There is a great need for the spreading of the gospel, but here]
I want to stress the divine truths....Actually, the gospel includes all
the divine truths....[The four Gospels] cover many things which
are altogether neglected and missed in today's Christianity.
When I say "the divine truths," I am referring to the New Testament economy of God, which is the gospel.

Paul called his entire...Epistle to the Romans "the gospel of
God" (1:1). The gospel of God in Romans does not include merely
the truth concerning justification by faith in the first four chapters. It also includes the Body of Christ in chapter twelve and the
local churches in chapter sixteen....According to my experience,
the gospel would be very deficient and poor without the church.
Actually, the entire New Testament is the gospel, from the first
page of Matthew through the last page of Revelation. The New
Testament as the gospel is typified by the Old Testament. Thus,
we may say that the gospel actually includes the entire Bible. (*The
World Situation and the Direction of the Lord's Move*, pp. 21-22)

Today's Reading

The first four seals unveil the new testament age, which is
an age of gospel preaching. Between Christ's ascension and His
coming back, the preaching of the gospel will continue. The other
main things—war, famine, and death—work together for the
advancement of the preaching of the gospel. God has a unique
purpose in this age—to have the gospel preached that the
church might be produced and built up for the fulfillment of His
eternal plan. We need to have this overall view. But the great
men on earth do not have this view. Not even the kings and the
presidents of the nations know what they are doing. But we

know. Everything these rulers do helps the preaching of the gospel. God is sovereign in this matter. (*Life-study of Revelation,* p. 241)

A crown [Rev. 6:2] signifies that the gospel has been crowned with the glory of Christ (2 Cor. 4:4). The gospel which we preach today has a crown, and this crown is the glory of Christ. We should not feel shameful when we preach the gospel. Rather, we should feel glorious….Those who preach the gospel become the riders of the white horse. (*The Prophecy of the Four "Sevens" in the Bible,* p. 29)

The spreading of the divine truths will bring in the Lord's restoration….The restoration will come because "the earth will be filled with the knowledge of Jehovah, / As water covers the sea" (Isa. 11:9). We have to speak for the Lord to bring in this restoration.

This is why we have to study these truths. Otherwise, we are not qualified to go to Europe. We should not go to speak to people in a superficial way. We may be able to speak John 3:16 to people….However, if someone asks us what eternal life is, we may not be able to tell them. It is possible to give fifteen messages on John 3:16. The first message can be concerning who God is, the second message can be on love, and the third message can be on the world. Then we can tell people how God gave His Son. God did not drop His Son down from the heavens to the earth. He gave His Son through incarnation. Then another message can be given on the only begotten Son. More can be said about what it means to perish and what it is to have eternal life. Message after message can be given on John 3:16.

We are not going there to preach to people in the traditional way, but to talk to them about all the divine truths. Through our speaking, some will be solidly saved. If we speak the deeper truths in John 3:16 to them, they will never forget this verse. May the Lord burden us to learn the divine truths and to spread them everywhere for His recovery and restoration. (*The World Situation and the Direction of the Lord's Move,* pp. 31-32)

Further Reading: The World Situation and the Direction of the Lord's Move, chs. 2-3; *The World Situation and God's Move,* ch. 7

Enlightenment and inspiration: _____

_____

_____

_____

Hymns, #1294

1   Come let us speak till the kingdom of the
       Lord comes down.
    Yes, let us speak till the kingdom of the
       Lord comes down.
     Why hold your peace?
     The Word release.
    Let us speak until the kingdom of the Lord
       comes down.

2   Oh, loose the Word! It shall not return
       unto Him void.
    Yes, loose the Word! It shall not return
       unto Him void.
     Let's sow the seed,
     This is our need;
    Loose the Word, and it shall not return
       unto Him void!

3   It's gospel time! Let us spread the gospel
       all around.
    Yes, gospel time! We will never fear the
       people's frown!
     God's done His work;
     Let us not shirk;
    We're but pilgrims here, and we'll not fear
       the people's frown!

4   If we will speak, Christ will witness in the
       hearts of men.
    If we will speak, Christ will witness in the
       hearts of men.
     Tell every man,
     Win all we can.
    Through our speaking, Christ is speaking
       in the hearts of men!

5   The harvest's ripe! We are preaching the
       full gospel now!
    The fields are white! We are preaching the
       full gospel now!
     For this men search—
     Christ and the church!
    Let us reap the harvest, preaching the
       full gospel now!

Composition for prophecy with main point and sub-points: _____

_____

_____

_____

_____

_____

_____

_____

_____

_____

_____

_____

_____

_____

_____

_____

_____

_____

_____

_____

_____

_____

_____

_____

_____

_____

_____

_____

_____

_____

_____

_____

_____

Reading Schedule for the Recovery Version of the Old Testament with Footnotes

Wk.	Lord's Day	Monday	Tuesday	Wednesday	Thursday	Friday	Saturday
1	☐ Gen 1:1-5	☐ 1:6-23	☐ 1:24-31	☐ 2:1-9	☐ 2:10-25	☐ 3:1-13	☐ 3:14-24
2	☐ 4:1-26	☐ 5:1-32	☐ 6:1-22	☐ 7:1—8:3	☐ 8:4-22	☐ 9:1-29	☐ 10:1-32
3	☐ 11:1-32	☐ 12:1-20	☐ 13:1-18	☐ 14:1-24	☐ 15:1-21	☐ 16:1-16	☐ 17:1-27
4	☐ 18:1-33	☐ 19:1-38	☐ 20:1-18	☐ 21:1-34	☐ 22:1-24	☐ 23:1—24:27	☐ 24:28-67
5	☐ 25:1-34	☐ 26:1-35	☐ 27:1-46	☐ 28:1-22	☐ 29:1-35	☐ 30:1-43	☐ 31:1-55
6	☐ 32:1-32	☐ 33:1—34:31	☐ 35:1-29	☐ 36:1-43	☐ 37:1-36	☐ 38:1—39:23	☐ 40:1—41:13
7	☐ 41:14-57	☐ 42:1-38	☐ 43:1-34	☐ 44:1-34	☐ 45:1-28	☐ 46:1-34	☐ 47:1-31
8	☐ 48:1-22	☐ 49:1-15	☐ 49:16-33	☐ 50:1-26	☐ Exo 1:1-22	☐ 2:1-25	☐ 3:1-22
9	☐ 4:1-31	☐ 5:1-23	☐ 6:1-30	☐ 7:1-25	☐ 8:1-32	☐ 9:1-35	☐ 10:1-29
10	☐ 11:1-10	☐ 12:1-14	☐ 12:15-36	☐ 12:37-51	☐ 13:1-22	☐ 14:1-31	☐ 15:1-27
11	☐ 16:1-36	☐ 17:1-16	☐ 18:1-27	☐ 19:1-25	☐ 20:1-26	☐ 21:1-36	☐ 22:1-31
12	☐ 23:1-33	☐ 24:1-18	☐ 25:1-22	☐ 25:23-40	☐ 26:1-14	☐ 26:15-37	☐ 27:1-21
13	☐ 28:1-21	☐ 28:22-43	☐ 29:1-21	☐ 29:22-46	☐ 30:1-10	☐ 30:11-38	☐ 31:1-17
14	☐ 31:18—32:35	☐ 33:1-23	☐ 34:1-35	☐ 35:1-35	☐ 36:1-38	☐ 37:1-29	☐ 38:1-31
15	☐ 39:1-43	☐ 40:1-38	☐ Lev 1:1-17	☐ 2:1-16	☐ 3:1-17	☐ 4:1-35	☐ 5:1-19
16	☐ 6:1-30	☐ 7:1-38	☐ 8:1-36	☐ 9:1-24	☐ 10:1-20	☐ 11:1-47	☐ 12:1-8
17	☐ 13:1-28	☐ 13:29-59	☐ 14:1-18	☐ 14:19-32	☐ 14:33-57	☐ 15:1-33	☐ 16:1-17
18	☐ 16:18-34	☐ 17:1-16	☐ 18:1-30	☐ 19:1-37	☐ 20:1-27	☐ 21:1-24	☐ 22:1-33
19	☐ 23:1-22	☐ 23:23-44	☐ 24:1-23	☐ 25:1-23	☐ 25:24-55	☐ 26:1-24	☐ 26:25-46
20	☐ 27:1-34	☐ Num 1:1-54	☐ 2:1-34	☐ 3:1-51	☐ 4:1-49	☐ 5:1-31	☐ 6:1-27
21	☐ 7:1-41	☐ 7:42-88	☐ 7:89—8:26	☐ 9:1-23	☐ 10:1-36	☐ 11:1-35	☐ 12:1—13:33
22	☐ 14:1-45	☐ 15:1-41	☐ 16:1-50	☐ 17:1—18:7	☐ 18:8-32	☐ 19:1-22	☐ 20:1-29
23	☐ 21:1-35	☐ 22:1-41	☐ 23:1-30	☐ 24:1-25	☐ 25:1-18	☐ 26:1-65	☐ 27:1-23
24	☐ 28:1-31	☐ 29:1-40	☐ 30:1—31:24	☐ 31:25-54	☐ 32:1-42	☐ 33:1-56	☐ 34:1-29
25	☐ 35:1-34	☐ 36:1-13	☐ Deut 1:1-46	☐ 2:1-37	☐ 3:1-29	☐ 4:1-49	☐ 5:1-33

Reading Schedule for the Recovery Version of the Old Testament with Footnotes

Wk.	Lord's Day	Monday	Tuesday	Wednesday	Thursday	Friday	Saturday
27	☐ 14:22—15:23	☐ 16:1-22	☐ 17:1—18:8	☐ 18:9—19:21	☐ 20:1—21:17	☐ 21:18—22:30	☐ 23:1-25
28	☐ 24:1-22	☐ 25:1-19	☐ 26:1-19	☐ 27:1-26	☐ 28:1-68	☐ 29:1-29	☐ 30:1—31:29
29	☐ 31:30—32:52	☐ 33:1-29	☐ 34:1-12	☐ Josh 1:1-18	☐ 2:1-24	☐ 3:1-17	☐ 4:1-24
30	☐ 5:1-15	☐ 6:1-27	☐ 7:1-26	☐ 8:1-35	☐ 9:1-27	☐ 10:1-43	☐ 11:1—12:24
31	☐ 13:1-33	☐ 14:1—15:63	☐ 16:1—18:28	☐ 19:1-51	☐ 20:1—21:45	☐ 22:1-34	☐ 23:1—24:33
32	☐ Judg 1:1-36	☐ 2:1-23	☐ 3:1-31	☐ 4:1-24	☐ 5:1-31	☐ 6:1-40	☐ 7:1-25
33	☐ 8:1-35	☐ 9:1-57	☐ 10:1—11:40	☐ 12:1—13:25	☐ 14:1—15:20	☐ 16:1-31	☐ 17:1—18:31
34	☐ 19:1-30	☐ 20:1-48	☐ 21:1-25	☐ Ruth 1:1-22	☐ 2:1-23	☐ 3:1-18	☐ 4:1-22
35	☐ 1 Sam 1:1-28	☐ 2:1-36	☐ 3:1—4:22	☐ 5:1—6:21	☐ 7:1—8:22	☐ 9:1-27	☐ 10:1—11:15
36	☐ 12:1—13:23	☐ 14:1-52	☐ 15:1-35	☐ 16:1-23	☐ 17:1-58	☐ 18:1-30	☐ 19:1-24
37	☐ 20:1-42	☐ 21:1—22:23	☐ 23:1—24:22	☐ 25:1-44	☐ 26:1-25	☐ 27:1—28:25	☐ 29:1—30:31
38	☐ 31:1-13	☐ 2 Sam 1:1-27	☐ 2:1-32	☐ 3:1-39	☐ 4:1—5:25	☐ 6:1-23	☐ 7:1-29
39	☐ 8:1—9:13	☐ 10:1—11:27	☐ 12:1-31	☐ 13:1-39	☐ 14:1-33	☐ 15:1—16:23	☐ 17:1—18:33
40	☐ 19:1-43	☐ 20:1—21:22	☐ 22:1-51	☐ 23:1-39	☐ 24:1-25	☐ 1 Kings 1:1-19	☐ 1:20-53
41	☐ 2:1-46	☐ 3:1-28	☐ 4:1-34	☐ 5:1—6:38	☐ 7:1-22	☐ 7:23-51	☐ 8:1-36
42	☐ 8:37-66	☐ 9:1-28	☐ 10:1-29	☐ 11:1-43	☐ 12:1-33	☐ 13:1-34	☐ 14:1-31
43	☐ 15:1-34	☐ 16:1—17:24	☐ 18:1-46	☐ 19:1-21	☐ 20:1-43	☐ 21:1—22:53	☐ 2 Kings 1:1-18
44	☐ 2:1—3:27	☐ 4:1-44	☐ 5:1—6:33	☐ 7:1-20	☐ 8:1-29	☐ 9:1-37	☐ 10:1-36
45	☐ 11:1—12:21	☐ 13:1—14:29	☐ 15:1-38	☐ 16:1-20	☐ 17:1-41	☐ 18:1-37	☐ 19:1-37
46	☐ 20:1—21:26	☐ 22:1-20	☐ 23:1-37	☐ 24:1—25:30	☐ 1 Chron 1:1-54	☐ 2:1—3:24	☐ 4:1—5:26
47	☐ 6:1-81	☐ 7:1-40	☐ 8:1-40	☐ 9:1-44	☐ 10:1—11:47	☐ 12:1-40	☐ 13:1—14:17
48	☐ 15:1—16:43	☐ 17:1-27	☐ 18:1—19:19	☐ 20:1—21:30	☐ 22:1—23:32	☐ 24:1—25:31	☐ 26:1-32
49	☐ 27:1-34	☐ 28:1—29:30	☐ 2 Chron 1:1-17	☐ 2:1—3:17	☐ 4:1—5:14	☐ 6:1-42	☐ 7:1—8:18
50	☐ 9:1—10:19	☐ 11:1—12:16	☐ 13:1—15:19	☐ 16:1—17:19	☐ 18:1—19:11	☐ 20:1-37	☐ 21:1—22:12
51	☐ 23:1—24:27	☐ 25:1—26:23	☐ 27:1—28:27	☐ 29:1-36	☐ 30:1—31:21	☐ 32:1-33	☐ 33:1—34:33
52	☐ 35:1—36:23	☐ Ezra 1:1-11	☐ 2:1-70	☐ 3:1—4:24	☐ 5:1—6:22	☐ 7:1-28	☐ 8:1-36

Reading Schedule for the Recovery Version of the Old Testament with Footnotes

Wk.	Lord's Day	Monday	Tuesday	Wednesday	Thursday	Friday	Saturday
53	9:1—10:44	Neh 1:1-11	2:1—3:32	4:1—5:19	6:1-19	7:1-73	8:1-18
54	9:1-20	9:21-38	10:1—11:36	12:1-47	13:1-31	Esth 1:1-22	2:1—3:15
55	4:1—5:14	6:1—7:10	8:1-17	9:1—10:3	Job 1:1-22	2:1—3:26	4:1—5:27
56	6:1—7:21	8:1—9:35	10:1—11:20	12:1—13:28	14:1—15:35	16:1—17:16	18:1—19:29
57	20:1—21:34	22:1—23:17	24:1—25:6	26:1—27:23	28:1—29:25	30:1—31:40	32:1—33:33
58	34:1—35:16	36:1-33	37:1-24	38:1-41	39:1-30	40:1-24	41:1-34
59	42:1-17	Psa 1:1-6	2:1—3:8	4:1—6:10	7:1—8:9	9:1—10:18	11:1—15:5
60	16:1—17:15	18:1-50	19:1—21:13	22:1-31	23:1—24:10	25:1—27:14	28:1—30:12
61	31:1—32:11	33:1—34:22	35:1—36:12	37:1-40	38:1—39:13	40:1—41:13	42:1—43:5
62	44:1-26	45:1-17	46:1—48:14	49:1—50:23	51:1—52:9	53:1—55:23	56:1—58:11
63	59:1—61:8	62:1—64:10	65:1—67:7	68:1-35	69:1—70:5	71:1—72:20	73:1—74:23
64	75:1—77:20	78:1-72	79:1—81:16	82:1—84:12	85:1—87:7	88:1—89:52	90:1—91:16
65	92:1—94:23	95:1—97:12	98:1—101:8	102:1—103:22	104:1—105:45	106:1-48	107:1-43
66	108:1—109:31	110:1—112:10	113:1—115:18	116:1—118:29	119:1-32	119:33-72	119:73-120
67	119:121-176	120:1—124:8	125:1—128:6	129:1—132:18	133:1—135:21	136:1—138:8	139:1—140:13
68	141:1—144:15	145:1—147:20	148:1—150:6	Prov 1:1-33	2:1—3:35	4:1—5:23	6:1-35
69	7:1—8:36	9:1—10:32	11:1—12:28	13:1—14:35	15:1-33	16:1-33	17:1-28
70	18:1-24	19:1—20:30	21:1—22:29	23:1—3:22	24:1—25:28	26:1—27:27	28:1—29:27
71	30:1-33	31:1-31	Eccl 1:1-18	2:1—3:22	4:1—5:20	6:1—7:29	8:1—9:18
72	10:1—11:10	12:1-14	S.S 1:1-8	1:9-17	2:1-17	3:1-11	4:1-8
73	4:9-16	5:1-16	6:1-13	7:1-13	8:1-14	Isa 1:1-11	1:12-31
74	2:1-22	3:1-26	4:1-6	5:1-30	6:1-13	7:1-25	8:1-22
75	9:1-21	10:1-34	11:1—12:6	13:1-22	14:1-14	14:15-32	15:1—16:14
76	17:1—18:7	19:1-25	20:1—21:17	22:1-25	23:1-18	24:1-23	25:1-12
77	26:1—21	27:1-13	28:1-29	29:1-24	30:1-33	31:1—32:20	33:1-24

Reading Schedule for the Recovery Version of the Old Testament with Footnotes

Wk.	Lord's Day	Monday	Tuesday	Wednesday	Thursday	Friday	Saturday
79	☐ 42:1-25	☐ 43:1-28	☐ 44:1-28	☐ 45:1-25	☐ 46:1-13	☐ 47:1-15	☐ 48:1-22
80	☐ 49:1-13	☐ 49:14-26	☐ 50:1—51:23	☐ 52:1-15	☐ 53:1-12	☐ 54:1-17	☐ 55:1-13
81	☐ 56:1-12	☐ 57:1-21	☐ 58:1-14	☐ 59:1-21	☐ 60:1-22	☐ 61:1-11	☐ 62:1-12
82	☐ 63:1-19	☐ 64:1-12	☐ 65:1-25	☐ 66:1-24	☐ Jer 1:1-19	☐ 2:1-19	☐ 2:20-37
83	☐ 3:1-25	☐ 4:1-31	☐ 5:1-31	☐ 6:1-30	☐ 7:1-34	☐ 8:1-22	☐ 9:1-26
84	☐ 10:1-25	☐ 11:1—12:17	☐ 13:1-27	☐ 14:1-22	☐ 15:1-21	☐ 16:1—17:27	☐ 18:1-23
85	☐ 19:1—20:18	☐ 21:1—22:30	☐ 23:1-40	☐ 24:1—25:38	☐ 26:1—27:22	☐ 28:1—29:32	☐ 30:1-24
86	☐ 31:1-23	☐ 31:24-40	☐ 32:1-44	☐ 33:1-26	☐ 34:1-22	☐ 35:1-19	☐ 36:1-32
87	☐ 37:1-21	☐ 38:1-28	☐ 39:1—40:16	☐ 41:1—42:22	☐ 43:1—44:30	☐ 45:1—46:28	☐ 47:1—48:16
88	☐ 48:17-47	☐ 49:1-22	☐ 49:23-39	☐ 50:1-27	☐ 50:28-46	☐ 51:1-27	☐ 51:28-64
89	☐ 52:1-34	☐ Lam 1:1-22	☐ 2:1-22	☐ 3:1-39	☐ 3:40-66	☐ 4:1-22	☐ 5:1-22
90	☐ Ezek 1:1-14	☐ 1:15-28	☐ 2:1—3:27	☐ 4:1—5:17	☐ 6:1—7:27	☐ 8:1—9:11	☐ 10:1—11:25
91	☐ 12:1—13:23	☐ 14:1—15:8	☐ 16:1-63	☐ 17:1—18:32	☐ 19:1-14	☐ 20:1-49	☐ 21:1-32
92	☐ 22:1-31	☐ 23:1-49	☐ 24:1-27	☐ 25:1—26:21	☐ 27:1-36	☐ 28:1-26	☐ 29:1—30:26
93	☐ 31:1—32:32	☐ 33:1-33	☐ 34:1-31	☐ 35:1—36:21	☐ 36:22-38	☐ 37:1-28	☐ 38:1—39:29
94	☐ 40:1-27	☐ 40:28-49	☐ 41:1-26	☐ 42:1—43:27	☐ 44:1-31	☐ 45:1-25	☐ 46:1-24
95	☐ 47:1-23	☐ 48:1-35	☐ Dan 1:1-21	☐ 2:1-30	☐ 2:31-49	☐ 3:1-30	☐ 4:1-37
96	☐ 5:1-31	☐ 6:1-28	☐ 7:1-12	☐ 7:13-28	☐ 8:1-27	☐ 9:1-27	☐ 10:1-21
97	☐ 11:1-22	☐ 11:23-45	☐ 12:1-13	☐ Hosea 1:1-11	☐ 2:1-23	☐ 3:1—4:19	☐ 5:1-15
98	☐ 6:1-11	☐ 7:1-16	☐ 8:1-14	☐ 9:1-17	☐ 10:1-15	☐ 11:1-12	☐ 12:1-14
99	☐ 13:1—14:9	☐ Joel 1:1-20	☐ 2:1-16	☐ 2:17-32	☐ 3:1-21	☐ Amos 1:1-15	☐ 2:1-16
100	☐ 3:1-15	☐ 4:1—5:27	☐ 6:1—7:17	☐ 8:1—9:15	☐ Obad 1-21	☐ Jonah 1:1-17	☐ 2:1—4:11
101	☐ Micah 1:1-16	☐ 2:1—3:12	☐ 4:1—5:15	☐ 6:1—7:20	☐ Nahum 1:1-15	☐ 2:1—3:19	☐ Hab 1:1-17
102	☐ 2:1-20	☐ 3:1-19	☐ Zeph 1:1-18	☐ 2:1-15	☐ 3:1-20	☐ Hag 1:1-15	☐ 2:1-23
103	☐ Zech 1:1-21	☐ 2:1-13	☐ 3:1-10	☐ 4:1-14	☐ 5:1—6:15	☐ 7:1—8:23	☐ 9:1-17
104	☐ 10:1—11:17	☐ 12:1—13:9	☐ 14:1-21	☐ Mal 1:1-14	☐ 2:1-17	☐ 3:1-18	☐ 4:1-6

Reading Schedule for the Recovery Version of the New Testament with Footnotes

Wk.	Lord's Day	Monday	Tuesday	Wednesday	Thursday	Friday	Saturday
1	☐ Matt 1:1-2	☐ 1:3-7	☐ 1:8-17	☐ 1:18-25	☐ 2:1-23	☐ 3:1-6	☐ 3:7-17
2	☐ 4:1-11	☐ 4:12-25	☐ 5:1-4	☐ 5:5-12	☐ 5:13-20	☐ 5:21-26	☐ 5:27-48
3	☐ 6:1-8	☐ 6:9-18	☐ 6:19-34	☐ 7:1-12	☐ 7:13-29	☐ 8:1-13	☐ 8:14-22
4	☐ 8:23-34	☐ 9:1-13	☐ 9:14-17	☐ 9:18-34	☐ 9:35—10:5	☐ 10:6-25	☐ 10:26-42
5	☐ 11:1-15	☐ 11:16-30	☐ 12:1-14	☐ 12:15-32	☐ 12:33-42	☐ 12:43—13:2	☐ 13:3-12
6	☐ 13:13-30	☐ 13:31-43	☐ 13:44-58	☐ 14:1-13	☐ 14:14-21	☐ 14:22-36	☐ 15:1-20
7	☐ 15:21-31	☐ 15:32-39	☐ 16:1-12	☐ 16:13-20	☐ 16:21-28	☐ 17:1-13	☐ 17:14-27
8	☐ 18:1-14	☐ 18:15-22	☐ 18:23-35	☐ 19:1-15	☐ 19:16-30	☐ 20:1-16	☐ 20:17-34
9	☐ 21:1-11	☐ 21:12-22	☐ 21:23-32	☐ 21:33-46	☐ 22:1-22	☐ 22:23-33	☐ 22:34-46
10	☐ 23:1-12	☐ 23:13-39	☐ 24:1-14	☐ 24:15-31	☐ 24:32-51	☐ 25:1-13	☐ 25:14-30
11	☐ 25:31-46	☐ 26:1-16	☐ 26:17-35	☐ 26:36-46	☐ 26:47-64	☐ 26:65-75	☐ 27:1-26
12	☐ 27:27-44	☐ 27:45-56	☐ 27:57—28:15	☐ 28:16-20	☐ Mark 1:1	☐ 1:2-6	☐ 1:7-13
13	☐ 1:14-28	☐ 1:29-45	☐ 2:1-12	☐ 2:13-28	☐ 3:1-19	☐ 3:20-35	☐ 4:1-25
14	☐ 4:26-41	☐ 5:1-20	☐ 5:21-43	☐ 6:1-29	☐ 6:30-56	☐ 7:1-23	☐ 7:24-37
15	☐ 8:1-26	☐ 8:27—9:1	☐ 9:2-29	☐ 9:30-50	☐ 10:1-16	☐ 10:17-34	☐ 10:35-52
16	☐ 11:1-16	☐ 11:17-33	☐ 12:1-27	☐ 12:28-44	☐ 13:1-13	☐ 13:14-37	☐ 14:1-26
17	☐ 14:27-52	☐ 14:53-72	☐ 15:1-15	☐ 15:16-47	☐ 16:1-8	☐ 16:9-20	☐ Luke 1:1-4
18	☐ 1:5-25	☐ 1:26-46	☐ 1:47-56	☐ 1:57-80	☐ 2:1-8	☐ 2:9-20	☐ 2:21-39
19	☐ 2:40-52	☐ 3:1-20	☐ 3:21-38	☐ 4:1-13	☐ 4:14-30	☐ 4:31-44	☐ 5:1-26
20	☐ 5:27—6:16	☐ 6:17-38	☐ 6:39-49	☐ 7:1-17	☐ 7:18-23	☐ 7:24-35	☐ 7:36-50
21	☐ 8:1-15	☐ 8:16-25	☐ 8:26-39	☐ 8:40-56	☐ 9:1-17	☐ 9:18-26	☐ 9:27-36
22	☐ 9:37-50	☐ 9:51-62	☐ 10:1-11	☐ 10:12-24	☐ 10:25-37	☐ 10:38-42	☐ 11:1-13
23	☐ 11:14-26	☐ 11:27-36	☐ 11:37-54	☐ 12:1-12	☐ 12:13-21	☐ 12:22-34	☐ 12:35-48
24	☐ 12:49-59	☐ 13:1-9	☐ 13:10-17	☐ 13:18-30	☐ 13:31—14:6	☐ 14:7-14	☐ 14:15-24
25	☐ 14:25-35	☐ 15:1-10	☐ 15:11-21	☐ 15:22-32	☐ 16:1-13	☐ 16:14-22	☐ 16:23-31

Reading Schedule for the Recovery Version of the New Testament with Footnotes

Wk.	Lord's Day	Monday	Tuesday	Wednesday	Thursday	Friday	Saturday
27	☐ Luke 19:28-48	☐ 20:1-19	☐ 20:20-38	☐ 20:39—21:4	☐ 21:5-27	☐ 21:28-38	☐ 22:1-20
28	☐ 22:21-38	☐ 22:39-54	☐ 22:55-71	☐ 23:1-43	☐ 23:44-56	☐ 24:1-12	☐ 24:13-35
29	☐ 24:36-53	☐ John 1:1-13	☐ 1:14-18	☐ 1:19-34	☐ 1:35-51	☐ 2:1-11	☐ 2:12-22
30	☐ 2:23—3:13	☐ 3:14-21	☐ 3:22-36	☐ 4:1-14	☐ 4:15-26	☐ 4:27-42	☐ 4:43-54
31	☐ 5:1-16	☐ 5:17-30	☐ 5:31-47	☐ 6:1-15	☐ 6:16-31	☐ 6:32-51	☐ 6:52-71
32	☐ 7:1-9	☐ 7:10-24	☐ 7:25-36	☐ 7:37-52	☐ 7:53—8:11	☐ 8:12-27	☐ 8:28-44
33	☐ 8:45-59	☐ 9:1-13	☐ 9:14-34	☐ 9:35—10:9	☐ 10:10-30	☐ 10:31—11:4	☐ 11:5-22
34	☐ 11:23-40	☐ 11:41-57	☐ 12:1-11	☐ 12:12-24	☐ 12:25-36	☐ 12:37-50	☐ 13:1-11
35	☐ 13:12-30	☐ 13:31-38	☐ 14:1-6	☐ 14:7-20	☐ 14:21-31	☐ 15:1-11	☐ 15:12-27
36	☐ 16:1-15	☐ 16:16-33	☐ 17:1-5	☐ 17:6-13	☐ 17:14-24	☐ 17:25—18:11	☐ 18:12-27
37	☐ 18:28-40	☐ 19:1-16	☐ 19:17-30	☐ 19:31-42	☐ 20:1-13	☐ 20:14-18	☐ 20:19-22
38	☐ 20:23-31	☐ 21:1-14	☐ 21:15-22	☐ 21:23-25	☐ Acts 1:1-8	☐ 1:9-14	☐ 1:15-26
39	☐ 2:1-13	☐ 2:14-21	☐ 2:22-36	☐ 2:37-41	☐ 2:42-47	☐ 3:1-18	☐ 3:19—4:22
40	☐ 4:23-37	☐ 5:1-16	☐ 5:17-32	☐ 5:33-42	☐ 6:1—7:1	☐ 7:2-29	☐ 7:30-60
41	☐ 8:1-13	☐ 8:14-25	☐ 8:26-40	☐ 9:1-19	☐ 9:20-43	☐ 10:1-16	☐ 10:17-33
42	☐ 10:34-48	☐ 11:1-18	☐ 11:19-30	☐ 12:1-25	☐ 13:1-12	☐ 13:13-43	☐ 13:44—14:5
43	☐ 14:6-28	☐ 15:1-12	☐ 15:13-34	☐ 15:35—16:5	☐ 16:6-18	☐ 16:19-40	☐ 17:1-18
44	☐ 17:19-34	☐ 18:1-17	☐ 18:18-28	☐ 19:1-20	☐ 19:21-41	☐ 20:1-12	☐ 20:13-38
45	☐ 21:1-14	☐ 21:15-26	☐ 21:27-40	☐ 22:1-21	☐ 22:22-29	☐ 22:30—23:11	☐ 23:12-15
46	☐ 23:16-30	☐ 23:31—24:21	☐ 24:22—25:5	☐ 25:6-27	☐ 26:1-13	☐ 26:14-32	☐ 27:1-26
47	☐ 27:27—28:10	☐ 28:11-22	☐ 28:23-31	☐ Rom 1:1-2	☐ 1:3-7	☐ 1:8-17	☐ 1:18-25
48	☐ 1:26—2:10	☐ 2:11-29	☐ 3:1-20	☐ 3:21-31	☐ 4:1-12	☐ 4:13-25	☐ 5:1-11
49	☐ 5:12-17	☐ 5:18—6:5	☐ 6:6-11	☐ 6:12-23	☐ 7:1-12	☐ 7:13-25	☐ 8:1-2
50	☐ 8:3-6	☐ 8:7-13	☐ 8:14-25	☐ 8:26-39	☐ 9:1-18	☐ 9:19—10:3	☐ 10:4-15
51	☐ 10:16—11:10	☐ 11:11-22	☐ 11:23-36	☐ 12:1-3	☐ 12:4-21	☐ 13:1-14	☐ 14:1-12
52	☐ 14:13-23	☐ 15:1-13	☐ 15:14-33	☐ 16:1-5	☐ 16:6-24	☐ 16:25-27	☐ 1 Cor 1:1-4

Reading Schedule for the Recovery Version of the New Testament with Footnotes

Wk.		Lord's Day		Monday		Tuesday		Wednesday		Thursday		Friday		Saturday
53	☐	1 Cor 1:5-9	☐	1:10-17	☐	1:18-31	☐	2:1-5	☐	2:6-10	☐	2:11-16	☐	3:1-9
54	☐	3:10-13	☐	3:14-23	☐	4:1-9	☐	4:10-21	☐	5:1-13	☐	6:1-11	☐	6:12-20
55	☐	7:1-16	☐	7:17-24	☐	7:25-40	☐	8:1-13	☐	9:1-15	☐	9:16-27	☐	10:1-4
56	☐	10:5-13	☐	10:14-33	☐	11:1-6	☐	11:7-16	☐	11:17-26	☐	11:27-34	☐	12:1-11
57	☐	12:12-22	☐	12:23-31	☐	13:1-13	☐	14:1-12	☐	14:13-25	☐	14:26-33	☐	14:34-40
58	☐	15:1-19	☐	15:20-28	☐	15:29-34	☐	15:35-49	☐	15:50-58	☐	16:1-9	☐	16:10-24
59	☐	2 Cor 1:1-4	☐	1:5-14	☐	1:15-22	☐	1:23—2:11	☐	2:12-17	☐	3:1-6	☐	3:7-11
60	☐	3:12-18	☐	4:1-6	☐	4:7-12	☐	4:13-18	☐	5:1-8	☐	5:9-15	☐	5:16-21
61	☐	6:1-13	☐	6:14—7:4	☐	7:5-16	☐	8:1-15	☐	8:16-24	☐	9:1-15	☐	10:1-6
62	☐	10:7-18	☐	11:1-15	☐	11:16-33	☐	12:1-10	☐	12:11-21	☐	13:1-10	☐	13:11-14
63	☐	Gal 1:1-5	☐	1:6-14	☐	1:15-24	☐	2:1-13	☐	2:14-21	☐	3:1-4	☐	3:5-14
64	☐	3:15-22	☐	3:23-29	☐	4:1-7	☐	4:8-20	☐	4:21-31	☐	5:1-12	☐	5:13-21
65	☐	5:22-26	☐	6:1-10	☐	6:11-15	☐	6:16-18	☐	Eph 1:1-3	☐	1:4-6	☐	1:7-10
66	☐	1:11-14	☐	1:15-18	☐	1:19-23	☐	2:1-5	☐	2:6-10	☐	2:11-14	☐	2:15-18
67	☐	2:19-22	☐	3:1-7	☐	3:8-13	☐	3:14-18	☐	3:19-21	☐	4:1-4	☐	4:5-10
68	☐	4:11-16	☐	4:17-24	☐	4:25-32	☐	5:1-10	☐	5:11-21	☐	5:22-26	☐	5:27-33
69	☐	6:1-9	☐	6:10-14	☐	6:15-18	☐	6:19-24	☐	Phil 1:1-7	☐	1:8-18	☐	1:19-26
70	☐	1:27—2:4	☐	2:5-11	☐	2:12-16	☐	2:17-30	☐	3:1-6	☐	3:7-11	☐	3:12-16
71	☐	3:17-21	☐	4:1-9	☐	4:10-23	☐	Col 1:1-8	☐	1:9-13	☐	1:14-23	☐	1:24-29
72	☐	2:1-7	☐	2:8-15	☐	2:16-23	☐	3:1-4	☐	3:5-15	☐	3:16-25	☐	4:1-18
73	☐	1 Thes 1:1-3	☐	1:4-10	☐	2:1-12	☐	2:13—3:5	☐	3:6-13	☐	4:1-10	☐	4:11—5:11
74	☐	5:12-28	☐	2 Thes 1:1-12	☐	2:1-17	☐	3:1-18	☐	1 Tim 1:1-2	☐	1:3-4	☐	1:5-14
75	☐	1:15-20	☐	2:1-7	☐	2:8-15	☐	3:1-13	☐	3:14—4:5	☐	4:6-16	☐	5:1-25
76	☐	6:1-10	☐	6:11-21	☐	2 Tim 1:1-10	☐	1:11-18	☐	2:1-15	☐	2:16-26	☐	3:1-13
77	☐	3:14—4:8	☐	4:9-22	☐	Titus 1:1-4	☐	1:5-16	☐	2:1-15	☐	3:1-8	☐	3:9-15

Reading Schedule for the Recovery Version of the New Testament with Footnotes

Wk.	Lord's Day	Monday	Tuesday	Wednesday	Thursday	Friday	Saturday
79	☐ Heb 3:1-6	☐ 3:7-19	☐ 4:1-9	☐ 4:10-13	☐ 4:14-16	☐ 5:1-10	☐ 5:11—6:3
80	☐ 6:4-8	☐ 6:9-20	☐ 7:1-10	☐ 7:11-28	☐ 8:1-6	☐ 8:7-13	☐ 9:1-4
81	☐ 9:5-14	☐ 9:15-28	☐ 10:1-18	☐ 10:19-28	☐ 10:29-39	☐ 11:1-6	☐ 11:7-19
82	☐ 11:20-31	☐ 11:32-40	☐ 12:1-2	☐ 12:3-13	☐ 12:14-17	☐ 12:18-26	☐ 12:27-29
83	☐ 13:1-7	☐ 13:8-12	☐ 13:13-15	☐ 13:16-25	☐ James 1:1-8	☐ 1:9-18	☐ 1:19-27
84	☐ 2:1-13	☐ 2:14-26	☐ 3:1-18	☐ 4:1-10	☐ 4:11-17	☐ 5:1-12	☐ 5:13-20
85	☐ 1 Pet 1:1-2	☐ 1:3-4	☐ 1:5	☐ 1:6-9	☐ 1:10-12	☐ 1:13-17	☐ 1:18-25
86	☐ 2:1-3	☐ 2:4-8	☐ 2:9-17	☐ 2:18-25	☐ 3:1-13	☐ 3:14-22	☐ 4:1-6
87	☐ 4:7-16	☐ 4:17-19	☐ 5:1-4	☐ 5:5-9	☐ 5:10-14	☐ 2 Pet 1:1-2	☐ 1:3-4
88	☐ 1:5-8	☐ 1:9-11	☐ 1:12-18	☐ 1:19-21	☐ 2:1-3	☐ 2:4-11	☐ 2:12-22
89	☐ 3:1-6	☐ 3:7-9	☐ 3:10-12	☐ 3:13-15	☐ 3:16	☐ 3:17-18	☐ 1 John 1:1-2
90	☐ 1:3-4	☐ 1:5	☐ 1:6	☐ 1:7	☐ 1:8-10	☐ 2:1-2	☐ 2:3-11
91	☐ 2:12-14	☐ 2:15-19	☐ 2:20-23	☐ 2:24-27	☐ 2:28-29	☐ 3:1-5	☐ 3:6-10
92	☐ 3:11-18	☐ 3:19-24	☐ 4:1-6	☐ 4:7-11	☐ 4:12-15	☐ 4:16—5:3	☐ 5:4-13
93	☐ 5:14-17	☐ 5:18-21	☐ 2 John 1:1-3	☐ 1:4-9	☐ 1:10-13	☐ 3 John 1:1-6	☐ 1:7-14
94	☐ Jude 1:1-4	☐ 1:5-10	☐ 1:11-19	☐ 1:20-25	☐ Rev 1:1-3	☐ 1:4-6	☐ 1:7-11
95	☐ 1:12-13	☐ 1:14-16	☐ 1:17-20	☐ 2:1-6	☐ 2:7	☐ 2:8-9	☐ 2:10-11
96	☐ 2:12-14	☐ 2:15-17	☐ 2:18-23	☐ 2:24-29	☐ 3:1-3	☐ 3:4-6	☐ 3:7-9
97	☐ 3:10-13	☐ 3:14-18	☐ 3:19-22	☐ 4:1-5	☐ 4:6-7	☐ 4:8-11	☐ 5:1-6
98	☐ 5:7-14	☐ 6:1-8	☐ 6:9-17	☐ 7:1-8	☐ 7:9-17	☐ 8:1-6	☐ 8:7-12
99	☐ 8:13—9:11	☐ 9:12-21	☐ 10:1-4	☐ 10:5-11	☐ 11:1-4	☐ 11:5-14	☐ 11:15-19
100	☐ 12:1-4	☐ 12:5-9	☐ 12:10-18	☐ 13:1-10	☐ 13:11-18	☐ 14:1-5	☐ 14:6-12
101	☐ 14:13-20	☐ 15:1-8	☐ 16:1-12	☐ 16:13-21	☐ 17:1-6	☐ 17:7-18	☐ 18:1-8
102	☐ 18:9—19:4	☐ 19:5-10	☐ 19:11-16	☐ 19:17-21	☐ 20:1-6	☐ 20:7-10	☐ 20:11-15
103	☐ 21:1	☐ 21:2	☐ 21:3-8	☐ 21:9-13	☐ 21:14-18	☐ 21:19-21	☐ 21:22-27
104	☐ 22:1	☐ 22:2	☐ 22:3-11	☐ 22:12-15	☐ 22:16-17	☐ 22:18-21	☐

Ezek.
1:15-16 And as I watched the living creatures, I saw a wheel upon the earth beside the living creatures, for *each of* their four faces. The appearance of the wheels and their workmanship were like the sight of beryl. And the four of them had one likeness; that is, their appearance and their workmanship were as it were a wheel within a wheel.

Date _____

Ezek.
1:13-14 As for the likeness of the living creatures, their appearance was like burning coals of fire, like the appearance of torches; the fire went to and fro among the living creatures, and the fire was bright; and out of the fire went forth lightning. And the living creatures ran to and fro like the appearance of a lightning bolt.

Date _____

1:11-12 upward; two *wings* of each were joined one to another, and two covered their bodies. And each went straight forward; wherever the Spirit was to go, they went; they did not turn as they went.
1 Cor.
12:9 To a different one faith in the same Spirit, and to another gifts of healing in the one Spirit.

Date _____

Week 1 — Day 3   Today's verses

Ezek.
1:5 And from the midst of it *there* came the likeness of four living creatures. And this was their appearance: They had the likeness of a man.

Psa.
8:4-5 What is mortal man, that You remember him, and the son of man, that You visit him? You have made Him a little lower than angels and have crowned Him with glory and honor.

Date _____

Week 1 — Day 2   Today's verses

Deut.
4:24 For Jehovah your God is a consuming fire, a jealous God.
Eph.
3:17 That Christ may make His home in your hearts through faith....
21 To Him be the glory in the church and in Christ Jesus unto all the generations forever and ever. Amen.

Date _____

Week 1 — Day 1   Today's verses

Ezek.
1:4 And I looked, and there came a storm wind from the north, a great cloud and a fire flashing incessantly; and there was a brightness around it, and from the midst of it there was *something* like the sight of electrum, from the midst of the fire.
Exo.
40:34 Then the cloud covered the Tent of Meeting, and the glory of Jehovah filled the tabernacle.

Date _____

John 15:12 one another even as I have loved you.
16-17 You did not choose Me, but I chose you, and I set you that you should go forth and bear fruit and *that* your fruit should remain, that whatever you ask the Father in My name, He may give you. These things I command you that you may love one another.

Date _____

Week 2 — Day 1   Today's verses

John 15:1-2 I am the true vine, and My Father is the husbandman. Every branch in Me that does not bear fruit, He takes it away; and every *branch* that bears fruit, He prunes it that it may bear more fruit.

Col. 2:9 ...In Him dwells all the fullness of the Godhead bodily.

Date _____

---

1 John 1:3 That which we have seen and heard we report also to you that you also may have fellowship with us, and indeed our fellowship is with the Father and with His Son Jesus Christ.
7 But if we walk in the light as He is in the light, we have fellowship with one another...

1 Cor. 1:9 God is faithful, through whom you were called into the fellowship of His Son, Jesus Christ our Lord.

Date _____

Week 2 — Day 2   Today's verses

John 15:4-5 Abide in Me and I in you. As the branch cannot bear fruit of itself unless it abides in the vine, so neither *can* you unless you abide in Me. I am the vine; you are the branches. He who abides in Me and I in him, he bears much fruit; for apart from Me you can do nothing.
8 In this is My Father glorified, that you bear much fruit and *so* you will become My disciples.

Date _____

Rom. 8:26-27 ...The Spirit also joins in to help *us* in our weakness, for we do not know for what we should pray as is fitting, but the Spirit Himself intercedes for *us* with groanings which cannot be uttered. But He who searches the hearts knows what the mind of the Spirit is, because He intercedes for the saints according to God.

Date _____

Week 2 — Day 3   Today's verses

John 3:15 That everyone who believes into Him may have eternal life.

Col. 3:4 When Christ our life is manifested, then you also will be manifested with Him in glory.

Phil. 4:13 I am able to do all things in Him who empowers me.

Date _____

...and there occurred in that day a great persecution against the church which was in Jerusalem; and all were scattered throughout the regions of Judea and Samaria, except the apostles.

8:1

9:31 So then the church throughout the whole of Judea and Galilee and Samaria had peace, being built up; and going on in the fear of the Lord and in the comfort of the Holy Spirit, it was multiplied.

Rom. Greet Prisca and Aquila, my fellow work-
16:3, 5 ers in Christ Jesus...and greet the church, which is in their house....

_____
Date

Week 3 — Day 1   Today's verses

Gen. And out of the ground Jehovah God
2:9 caused to grow every tree that is pleasant to the sight and good for food, as well as the tree of life in the middle of the garden and the tree of the knowledge of good and evil.

Rev. He who has an ear, let him hear what the
2:7 Spirit says to the churches. To him who overcomes, to him I will give to eat of the tree of life, which is in the Paradise of God.

_____
Date

Exo. And you shall make a lampstand of pure
25:31 gold. The lampstand with its base and its shaft shall be made of beaten work; its cups, its calyxes, and its blossom buds shall be of one piece with it.

Rev. Saying, What you see write in a scroll and
1:11-12 send it to the seven churches....And I turned to see the voice that spoke with me; and when I turned, I saw seven golden lampstands.

_____
Date

Week 3 — Day 2   Today's verses

Rev. And he showed me a river of water of life,
22:1-2 bright as crystal, proceeding out of the throne of God and of the Lamb in the middle of its street. And on this side and on that side of the river was the tree of life...

_____
Date

Eph. ...The Head, Christ, out from whom all
4:15-16 the Body, being joined together and being knit together through every joint of the rich supply and through the operation in the measure of each one part, causes the growth of the Body unto the building up of itself in love.

5:8 For you were once darkness but are now light in the Lord; walk as children of light.

_____
Date

Week 3 — Day 3   Today's verses

1 Cor. I planted, Apollos watered, but God
3:6-7 caused the growth. So then neither is he who plants anything nor he who waters, but God who causes the growth.

Col. ...Holding the Head, out from whom all
2:19 the Body, being richly supplied and knit together by means of the joints and sinews, grows with the growth of God.

_____
Date

Gen. 12:7 And Jehovah appeared to Abram and said, To your seed I will give this land. And there he built an altar to Jehovah who had appeared to him.

Gen. 13:18 And Abram moved his tent and came and dwelt by the oaks of Mamre, which are in Hebron, and there he built an altar to Jehovah.

Lev. 23:42-43 You shall dwell in booths seven days...so that your descendants may know that I made the children of Israel to dwell in booths when I brought them out of the land of Egypt...

Rev. 21:2-3 And I saw the holy city, New Jerusalem, coming down out of heaven from God...And I heard a loud voice out of the throne, saying, Behold, the tabernacle of God is with men...

Date

Week 4 — Day 2   Today's verses

Acts 7:2 And he said, Men, brothers and fathers, listen. The God of glory appeared to our father Abraham while he was in Mesopotamia, before he dwelt in Haran.

Gen. 15:6 And he believed Jehovah, and He accounted it to him as righteousness.

Heb. 11:10 For he eagerly waited for the city which has the foundations, whose Architect and Builder is God.

16 But as it is, they long after a better *country*, that is, a heavenly one. Therefore God is not ashamed of them, to be called their God, for He has prepared a city for them.

Date

Week 4 — Day 1   Today's verses

Gal. 3:7 Know then that they who are of faith, these are sons of Abraham.

Heb. 11:8-9 By faith Abraham, being called, obeyed to go out unto a place which he was to receive as an inheritance; and he went out, not knowing where he was going. By faith he dwelt as a foreigner in the land of promise as in a foreign *land*, making his home in tents with Isaac and Jacob, the fellow heirs of the same promise.

...of promise as in a foreign *land*, making his home in tents...

13 ...Confessing that they were strangers and sojourners on the earth.

Gen. 12:8 And he proceeded from there to the mountain on the east of Bethel and pitched his tent, with Bethel on the west and Ai on the east; and there he built an altar to Jehovah and called upon the name of Jehovah.

Date

... that I want you to know, brothers, that the things concerning me have turned out rather to the advancement of the gospel.

Phil. 1:12

22 But if I am to live in the flesh, if this to me is fruit for *my* work, then I do not know what I will choose.

Acts 1:8

But you shall receive power when the Holy Spirit comes upon you, and you shall be My witnesses both in Jerusalem and in all Judea and Samaria and unto the uttermost part of the earth.

2 Cor. 12:15

But I, I will most gladly spend and be utterly spent on behalf of your souls....

Phil. 1:23-25

But I am constrained between the two, having the desire to depart and be with Christ, for *this is* far better; but to remain in the flesh is more necessary for your sake. And being confident of this, I know that I will remain and continue with you all for your progress and joy of the faith.

Date

Date

Date

Week 5 — Day 1   Today's verses

Phil. 1:5-6

For your fellowship unto *the furtherance of* the gospel from the first day until now, being confident of this very thing, that He who has begun in you a good work will complete it until the day of Christ Jesus.

John 13:35

By this shall all men know that you are My disciples, if you have love for one another.

Week 5 — Day 2   Today's verses

Phil. 1:27

Only, conduct yourselves in a manner worthy of the gospel of Christ, that whether coming and seeing you or being absent, I may hear of the things concerning you, that you stand firm in one spirit, with one soul striving together *along* with the faith of the gospel.

Week 5 — Day 3   Today's verses

1 Thes. 1:3

Remembering unceasingly your work of faith and labor of love and endurance of hope in our Lord Jesus Christ, before our God and Father.

2 Thes. 3:5

And the Lord direct your hearts into the love of God and into the endurance of Christ.

Date

Date

Date

Eph. To me, less than the least of all saints, was
3:8-9 this grace given to announce to the Gentiles the unsearchable riches of Christ as the gospel and to enlighten all *that they may see* what the economy of the mystery is, which throughout the ages has been hidden in God, who created all things.

Today's verses

Date

17:26-27 men to dwell on all the face of the earth, determining beforehand *their* appointed seasons and the boundaries of their dwelling, that they might seek God, if perhaps they might grope for Him and find Him....

Rev. These will make war with the Lamb, and
17:14 the Lamb will overcome them, for He is Lord of lords and King of kings....

Date

Rev. And I saw when the Lamb opened one of
6:1-2 the seven seals....And I saw, and behold, a white horse; and he who sits on it had a bow; and a crown was given to him, and he went forth conquering and to conquer.

Matt. And this gospel of the kingdom will be
24:14 preached in the whole inhabited earth for a testimony to all the nations, and then the end will come.

Today's verses

Date

Week 6 — Day 1   **Today's verses**

Zech. ...Now your King comes to you. He is
9:9 righteous and bears salvation, lowly and riding upon a donkey....

13:1 In that day there will be an opened fountain for the house of David and for the inhabitants of Jerusalem, for sin and for impurity.

14:9 And Jehovah will be King over all the earth....

Date

Week 6 — Day 2   **Today's verses**

Zech. For here is the stone that I have set before
3:9 Joshua—upon one stone are seven eyes. I will engrave its engraving, declares Jehovah of hosts, and I will remove the iniquity of that land in one day.

1 Tim. ...The love of money is a root of all evils,
6:10 *because of* which some...have been led away from the faith and pierced themselves through with many pains.

6 But godliness with contentment is great gain.

Date

Week 6 — Day 3   **Today's verses**

Dan. ...A stone was cut out without hands, and
2:34-35 it struck the image at its feet of iron and clay and crushed them. Then the iron, the clay, the bronze, the silver, and the gold were crushed all at once, and they became like chaff from the summer threshing floors; and the wind carried them away so that no trace of them was found. And the stone that struck the image became a great mountain and filled the whole earth.

Date